Investment Wisdom

Investment Wisdom

Great Australian investors
share their stories

Brett Kelly

CLOWN
PUBLISHING

Clown Publishing
PO Box 1764, North Sydney NSW 2059, Australia
Telephone: (02) 9923 0800 Facsimile: (02) 9923 0888
Email: brett@brettkelly.com.au
www.brettkelly.com.au

First published January 2020

Every effort has been made by the editors and publisher to trace and
acknowledge copyright material. The publisher would be pleased to hear from
any copyright holders who have not been acknowledged.

**National Library of Australia
Catalogue-in-Publication data:**

Author	Kelly, Brett, 1974–
Title	Investment Wisdom: Great Australian investors share their stories / Brett Kelly.
ISBN	978-0-9807765-4-6 (hbk.)
ISBN	978-0-9807765-5-3 (pbk.)
Series:	Investment Wisdom ; No.1.
Subjects:	Entrepreneurship–Australia.
	Businesspeople–Australia.
	Entrepreneurship–Australia–Anecdotes.
	Businesspeople–Australia–Anecdotes.
Dewey Number:	338.04

Editorial Management Primary Ideas
Editor Katarina Kroslakova
Copy-Editor/Proofreader Ella Martin

Design Aleksandra Beare
Illustrations Aleksandra Beare
Pre-Media Ovato

Printing Toppan Security Printing Pte. Ltd., Singapore

10 9 8 7 6 5 4 3 2 1

General Advice Warning
This book may contain general advice. Any general advice provided has been
commented without taking into account your objectives, financial situation or
needs. Before acting on any advice, you should consider the appropriateness of
the advice with regard to your objectives, financial situation and needs.

This book is dedicated to my wife, Rebecca.

Her partnership with me has been focused, patient, long-term and has resulted in life's ultimate investment returns: our love, and our family with three precious children, Thomas, Nicholas and Audrey.

Contents

Kelly+Partners Scholars Foundation

The mission of the Kelly+Partners Scholars Foundation is to inspire business leadership for the 21st century.

Kelly+Partners Scholars provides scholarships to Year 11 students for a study trip to Israel to understand how innovation and technology can be drivers of positive social impact through business.

The full 100 per cent of proceeds from the sale of *Investment Wisdom* will be donated to the Kelly+Partners Scholars Foundation with the goal to sell 40,000 copies to raise $2 million that will allow 30 students per year for the next 100 years to be provided a scholarship.

Acknowledgements

This book, and the now four books that form a part of a series I commenced in 1998 (*Collective Wisdom, Universal Wisdom, Business Owners' Wisdom* and now *Investment Wisdom*) has been inspired by the long-running BBC documentary series, *Seven Up*.

In 2003, determined to remember to 'always be alive to life' and not to be one of those people who wanders unconsciously through life until death grabs them, I decided to emulate the *Seven Up* series and write a book every seven years. Each book would encompass what had been my focus over the previous seven years, and to an extent, set me up to continue that focus for the next seven years.

I believed this reflection would help me decide actively if I liked where I was and what I was doing.

Here is the current instalment.

I want to thank all the people who have helped with this book. These key people include Gary Chestney, Josh Thomas, Claudia Pan and Katarina Kroslakova and her publishing team.

In particular, my wife Rebecca and our children Thomas, Nicholas and Audrey are the often-unnoticed inspiration for all I do. I love you and want to thank you.

To my mum and dad, teachers and all who have inspired in me my relentless love of learning, thank you.

To my partners, colleagues and clients at Kelly+Partners, we love how we help others. Thank you for believing in our mission of how we can make a difference through our work.

And of course, my thanks also go to the great investment leaders for their generosity of time, spirit and energy when conducting these interviews with me. Without you and your teams, this book wouldn't exist.

Introduction

In my 2005 book, *Universal Wisdom*, I profiled seven people who had changed the world. One of those people, Warren Buffett, was to have a significant impact on my career. I have been reading about Buffett since 1991, when I was 17 years old. He struck me as not just a man of brilliant ideas but also one who had implemented those ideas with real commitment.

In 1991, Buffett wrote:

John Maynard Keynes, whose brilliance as a practicing investor matched his brilliance in thought, wrote a letter to a business associate, F. C. Scott, on August 15, 1934, that says it all: "As time goes on, I get more and more convinced that the right method in investment is to put fairly large sums into enterprises which one thinks one knows something about and in the management of which one thoroughly believes. It is a mistake to think that one limits one's risk by spreading too much between enterprises about which one knows little and has no reason for special confidence…One's knowledge and experience are definitely limited and there are seldom more than two or three enterprises at any given time in which I personally feel myself entitled to put full confidence."

Six years later, those words and a Buffett mantra would play a huge role in my own success.

When I lost an investment banking job in 1997, I had the realisation that I now had the freedom to choose my own path. As I wrote in the introduction to *Collective Wisdom*, I realised I did not want to live according to other people's expectations of a normal life for me and that whether you deal well with people is the ultimate determinant of your own happiness, meaning in life and success.

With that in mind, I embarked on a journey of ideas. In 1998, I published the first edition of *Collective Wisdom*; in 2005, it was *Universal Wisdom*, followed in 2012 by *Business Owners' Wisdom* and now, in 2019, *Investment Wisdom*. Every seven years, a new book.

This idea was inspired by the *Up* series of documentary films from British television. Beginning in 1964, they look in on the lives of 14 British women and men every seven years, starting from when they were children just 7 years old. To date, the series has featured nine episodes, covering 56 years. The 14 children who were chosen for the original show, *Seven Up*, were picked to represent Britain's various socioeconomic backgrounds back in 1964. The idea was that their class would determine their future. For each new documentary, the director, Michael Apted, films material from those of the 14 who choose to participate. The most recent instalment, 63 Up, premiered in the UK on 4 June 2019.

It is the most magnificent study of people and their progress over time. The late, revered film critic Roger Ebert called the series "an inspired, even noble, use of the film medium".

"To look at these films, as I have every seven years," Ebert wrote, "is to meditate on the astonishing fact that man is the only animal that knows it lives in time."

My effort, to date, is relatively modest; my first book was written the year I turned 23 and this year I turned 45. Why do I do it? Because by revealing my personal insights via this project, I hope that I can learn and share with others a growing understanding of life over time. But freedom to choose my own path has led me to do more than write. It has shaped my career in business as well. Warren Buffett and his world once again showed the way.

Focusing on the future forces you to think, I had heard Buffett say. Look at least 20 years down the line. He insisted on it. So when I started Kelly+Partners Chartered Accountants in 2006, I decided taxes were a good place to invest my efforts, because they would be with us for the foreseeable future.

And when it was time to determine exactly how my business should evolve, Warren's business partner, Charlie Munger, set the bar. Charlie is one of the world's wittiest and wisest men. He is also an investing legend. Many people don't know that his background is as a Harvard-trained lawyer and founder of his own law firm, Munger, Tolles & Olson. Over time, Charlie became a huge influence on me – and a challenge. Could I build my accounting firm as an investor would grow a business and ultimately become regarded as someone who could help others invest as well?

Since I founded Kelly+Partners in 2006, the implementation of my investment ideas has been influenced by distant mentors like Warren, Munger and Keynes. It centres on taking a concentrated position and investing all my talents, energy and financial resources to make a difference in the lives of my clients, team members and communities. My Pollyanna theory was that in doing great I could feel great, buoyed by the meaningfulness of the work, the relationships I formed and the people we helped – while making industry industry-leading returns. Was it possible? Or should I just agree with the miserable industry-leading voices that always told me what couldn't be done and how my views were too idealistic?

Off we went with KPG. We grew revenue by an average of 35 per cent annually for almost 14 consecutive years and listed on the ASX in 2017 as the 24th-largest firm in the country – 40 partners, 230 team members, 7000 clients and 14 locations. Our 'crazy' ideas have been well received and we've compounded the initial invested capital at 57 per cent a year over nearly 14 years.

I know that none of that success and fulfilment would've been possible without the access I've had to the inspiring example of great investors. This led to the bright idea for the concept and writing of Investment Wisdom. I wondered: Who are Australia's great investors here at home, who could show me their insights, wisdom and character in a face-to-face interview? As I had seen in my previous books, people enjoyed the opportunity to get an insight into people who were living their dreams. The chapters would be manageable reads that might inspire further research on someone who appealed to the reader in some way.

The process has been invigorating and refreshing, as you will see within these pages. The generosity with which people share their insights is normally in direct proportion to their competence and confidence in themselves. I would like to say thank-you to these generous people, who helped make this book possible.

Please enjoy and let me know any feedback.

Brett Kelly
brett.kelly@kellypartners.com.au

Stories

Charlie Aitken

Executive Director, CEO & Chief Investment Officer
at Aitken Investment Management

'Make them laugh, make them think, make them money.'

Charlie has more than 22 years of equity and futures market experience. His career experience includes being a Director and Head of Sydney Sales Trading for Citigroup, Executive Director and Partner of Southern Cross Equities, and Executive Director and Board Member of the ASX-listed Bell Financial Group. Charlie was the author of Ringing the Bell and Under the Southern Cross newsletters. He is an expert contributor to the Switzer Super Report and previously, Alan Kohler's Eureka Report. He appears frequently on Australian and global financial media as an expert on Australian equities and global macro-economic strategy.

He is best known for his high conviction and his top-down, bottom-up investment ideas formulated from consistently meeting with listed and unlisted companies, policy makers and regulators.

aimfunds.com.au/team

Interview

BRETT KELLY: I normally ask a question off the bat, which often gives a good answer. Motto, quote or thought that best summarises your approach to life?

CHARLIE AITKEN: Well, back in my stockbroking days, my professional motto was: 'Make them laugh, make them think, make them money.' You need humility; you need a bit of humour. You need to make people think. But, at the same time, I need to make returns for people. So, make them laugh, make them think and make them money still stands.

BK: Excellent. Did you grow up in Sydney?

CA: Yes, I was born in the tough streets of Vaucluse; that's where I was brought up. Investing was in my blood. My father John Aitken was the chief executive of Perpetual; he started the Perpetual Industrial Share Fund, which to this day, is still one of the most successful funds in Australian history.

'Investing was in my blood.'

Dad's influence was very much there, if only subliminally. I have two brothers and Dad would take us out on Sundays to give Mum a break. We'd go and look at chip pallet pools, train lines, and warehouses in Western Sydney. We didn't know it at the time, but Dad was doing his due diligence. It was great. That's how I invest now. You have to see assets, you have to keep ties, you have to meet with management. It's not unsurprising that my brothers are in investment markets too.

BK: And your education?

CA: I went to Sydney Grammar like my father and his father, but I did my first year of economics at Sydney University and then dropped out; that's where we differ.

Afterwards, Dad found out I was playing golf with his friends and decided that wasn't appropriate. I was betting money against them and winning a little. As a fund manager, he called in a favour from an old friend of his, a well-respected stockbroker called Eric Gale who worked at Ord Minnett. My first job was picking up traders' receipts from the floor of the Sydney Futures Exchange.

*'My first job was picking up traders' receipts from the floor
of the Sydney Futures Exchange.'*

My time on the Sydney Futures Exchange floor, which was the first few years
of my career, taught me more than any economics degree could have about the
realities of markets, about emotion and how people react to things, and forced
selling, forced buying. Everything, in fact. It was a wonderful entrée into markets
and investing.

From there on, I learned from my peers. The older guys in the market took
me under their wing at County NatWest and I learned from experience and
from observation. Early in my brokering career, I modelled myself on the hardest
working and most successful brokers in the firm. They were always at their desks
early: they worked hard, put in the longest hours, and generally got the best
returns for their clients and business. I still have that work ethic now.

BK: Where to after County NatWest?

CA: County NatWest was bought out by Solomon Brothers, who became City
Group, so I joined former colleagues at Southern Cross Equities, a boutique
brokering firm. It was the perfect position and I rode the entire mining cycle of
2003 to 2008 and beyond. Eventually, Bell Potter bought Southern Cross Equities,
where I worked for another five or six years before I decided it was time to switch
sides and actually look after people's money rather than just talk about money.

BK: When you started your own firm, what was the process?

CA: I'd been a shareholder in an unlisted public company at Southern Cross, with
a lot of guidance from management, the older guys and board members, but it's
fair to say, Brett, I underestimated the major challenge it would be.

In the first year of my new business – Aitken Investment Management (AIM)
– I totally underestimated the compliance regime; the infrastructure required;
the oversight required; and the capital investment required. I also underestimated
how hard it was to raise money without a track record. I may have had a track
record in stockbroking, but I had no such thing in actually managing money.
There were obviously people who would give you some money to have a go;
I called them the coalition of the willing.

From then on, it was really hard. I underestimated the cost, the scale –
everything – of the change. The idea for the business came from some of the
investors. I'd written investment newsletters for a long time, and daily notes, and

they had a pretty big following. Many of those people said: 'If you ever look after money, I'll give you some.'

So I thought I'd better do it properly. I had to set up proper infrastructure, get a proper team, proper balance sheet; everything had to be done properly. But when you do things properly, as you know, it's expensive. So you're digging this hole, digging this hole... I would call the first year of my business the Valley of Death. You've got to go through the Valley of Death in order to come out the other side and see how much you want it. It's a true test.

'You've got to go through the Valley of Death in order to come out the other side and see how much you want it. It's a true test.'

BK: Bernard Arnault says, 'Be pessimistic in the short term and optimistic in the long term.' He always asks, 'What can put me out of business today?'

CA: Yes. When I started the business, I paid off all debt, and made sure I saved. I made sure the business was ungeared and I was ungeared. If you start a small business, I don't think you can have high personal gearing or much personal gearing. I wanted to make good, clean decisions; long-term decisions about the business. So I proactively made sure my finances were in good order, so the business would be in good order.

BK: That was a good decision because in the first year, if you had geared yourself, it could have been gone.

CA: I understand how many businesses go in the first year. You've got a business plan, but its execution can be completely different to what you'd planned. A good decision helped me get through that first year. But the true test is, how much do you want it? It's not going quite according to plan. You've got a bit of staff turnover. You've picked some of the wrong people. The money you've raised is less than you thought. The cost of the business is higher than you thought. And suddenly you think, 'Why did I leave my well-paid salary?'

It was all care, no responsibility. But when you come out the other side and you realise you've got a good business, and you've got good clients, and you've got good staff, and you've got an idea. That's exciting. For me, that was the best part. The best part of this now is that we invest, and we try to buy the best companies in the world – and stick with them. That can be hard because the short term can be against you for whatever reason, but if you buy the best companies in the world, you'll be all right.

'If you buy the best companies in the world, you'll be all right.'

Thankfully, I've got good people with me and good business partners. My wife's been very supportive and very helpful as well.

My advice to others is to make sure you're using realistic budgets and have your own finances in order before you embark on something. I can see how quickly you can go in small business – everything takes longer and costs more. The rewards are there in a few years' time, but there are very, very few instant success stories. That's not the real world.

'There are very, very few instant success stories.
That's not the real world.'

BK: When it does happen, people don't often look at where that person started. Take Elon Musk, he's been in business for over 20 years. He started with PayPal and it's fair to say that his working weeks are the equivalent of three weeks of most people.

CA: Correct.

BK: So, he's probably worked 60 years to get where he has in 20 years. A guy like Zuckerberg was working 120 hours a week.

CA: My business motto, apart from make them laugh, make them think, make them money, is ROE: return on effort. I will put in as good an effort as anyone. I've got energy. I've got enthusiasm. I'm fit, I work as hard as anyone. I may not be the smartest guy, but I can put that energy in. So I want to see a return on that effort. Return on effort is measurable.

'Return on effort is measurable.'

BK: And it's reliable.

CA: Correct. And there is a strong return on effort. If you put in a concentrated, well-directed effort, if you're honest, you will get a return.

Too few people find out how hard they can go. Or how they can work or how concentrated they can work. They don't get to that point. You can probably only get to that point if you're self-employed. You're staring down the abyss. I've got children; this has to work.

'Too few people find out how hard they can go.'

BK: In our businesses, I set people up but it takes about 12 months to see it in their eyes, for them to have looked at their bank account, realise that there's no money in there and know that no-one else is putting it in there.

CA: Unless they put it in there with effort – it's a whole new world.

BK: But the animal that comes out the other side is also a whole new person, much more resilient.

CA: Correct. There's a moment in your life when you lose the ego and the show-off stuff. My goal is to protect and grow the wealth of my investors and provide my family with a good education and enduring living. I'll work as hard as I can to make that happen; it's not about me anymore.

BK: I read a book recently that talked about two of the eight, who shrunk their companies. Size is everything to blokes, but these guys were all about earnings per share, cash flow per share...

CA: And the dividends you pay out, yes.

BK: It's enduring forever if you do it that way. They didn't give any market guidance; they didn't do meetings with analysts; they never appeared on the cover of *Fortune* magazine. They just did the business, had great families, zero divorce rates – that type of stuff. A completely different set of values; a completely different view. They call them iconoclasts. Buffett is obviously the biggest example of that kind of person, but there are a whole school of people with those ideas – and they've all got returns that are better than anyone else's.

CA: No doubt I've worked hard in my life, but in the early years, I probably did think it was a bit of a pissing contest, but it's all meaningless. It's just moving past that stage. It frees you up to do what you want to do and be who you want to be. It's also part of growing up; you lose a bit of ego. It doesn't mean you lose the drive, but you realise it's all about looking after investors and family. Look, I'm self-

'I try to read as much as I can from people I respect in terms of investments and managing companies. Obviously, with the amount of information out there, you can read a huge amount.'

taught. I try to read as much as I can from people I respect in terms of investments and managing companies. Obviously, with the amount of information out there, you can read a huge amount.

BK: You can read, listen to or watch the best thinkers who ever lived.

CA: Yes. You can never do enough of that. In my opinion, most of what really well-regarded, proven people say is correct. I try to have as little to do with the day-to-day noise of the world as possible. The biggest money you make in investing is by buying great companies, or fast-growing companies, and holding on to them. The instantaneous 24-hour news cycle doesn't drive you toward that style of investing, but that's how you make the most money. So if I can avoid the noise that could make me sell one of those companies, or partially sell one of them, I will. You will always regret it.

BK: It's like property...

CA: Yes, I remember my first two houses. I should have just kept them.

BK: That's what they all say. I've never had a client sit in front of me and say, I wish I had sold that property. They always say, if I'd had the time or the money, I'd have kept every property I've ever bought.

CA: That goes back to one of my other beliefs: quality is always cheap. To me, irreplaceable assets, with population growth in the world and a bit of inflation, will almost always be worth more at some stage. It might be three years, five years, ten years, but it will be worth more.

BK: So, there's this great line that Steve Jobs delivered to Bernard Arnault, who helped him with the Apple Store: 'You've got an amazing company. I don't know if in 50 years anyone will be using my iPhone, but I do know they'll be drinking your Dom Pérignon.'

CA: Correct. The world is aspirational.

BK: The human spirit is aspirational.

CA: And it should be.

BK: So, your biggest mistakes in business, investing, life?

CA: I've made plenty of mistakes; I make them on a daily basis. It's about how you deal with them that matters. The one thing I do make sure of though is that I always play within the rules; that's never a mistake.

'I always play within the rules; that's never a mistake.'

I've made mistakes in judgement or investment mistakes, and I've underestimated the transition from being a salaried employee to a small business owner. It wasn't a fatal mistake, but it was high pressure. The business plan didn't evolve as I thought it would.

My biggest mistake in investing was not dealing with losses quick enough. You know you're wrong, deal with it, which means sell it. Another mistake is being tempted into stocks that might be moving in the short term, or attractive in the short term, but are not really your style. That also comes down to portfolio management; not betting on just one thing. Have a spread of assets, a spread of industries. Try to keep the quality high.

The biggest mistakes you make in investing are being short term; trying to be a trader. Don't be a trader.

BK: Are you an investor, or are you a trader?

CA: Well, they're completely different.

BK: Yes, a 100-metre sprint versus running an ultra-long marathon. Which brings me to my next question. The women don't get a pat on the back, but I know I couldn't have built my business without my wife. How have you and your wife made it work? I've met a lot of people who've made a lot of money, but have blown up their families...

CA: Well, that's one thing I won't do. The absolute number one thing to me is my wife, Ellie, and my young children. Business is second to that. I want healthy, happy children. I want to provide them with an expansive and interesting life. Ultimately, I think my job and my wife's job is to make sure our children fit into whatever world is ahead of us; that they can find a job and find the world interesting.

The family thing is really important, but don't get me wrong, that first year wasn't easy. It required a lot of hard work. I had a high profile, Ellie has a profile, it was pretty clear things didn't go well in the first six to twelve months. We had to stick together even tighter than ever; we pulled our heads in a little bit. It doesn't mean you've lost confidence, but you circle the wagons around what matters. Wife, children, that's about it. And you toughen up.

Ellie's been fantastic. She encouraged me to do this, and she knew it was a risk, but she's one of the biggest investors in the fund. She sits on the board, owns a big chunk of the business herself. We have our shareholdings in the business split down the middle; that's a good way to do things.

BK: You want her engaged.

CA: Absolutely. She's fully engaged. Her involvement in the business has been excellent. She's a very educated person, she's got three degrees, multiple experiences that are different to mine. But it hasn't been easy for us. Australia has been fantastic to me, and I love Australia, but the one thing I find very frustrating is that we are very quick to kick someone when they're even partially down. It's a terrible trait. The greatest trait in the world is kindness. When things are going wrong, you hope people will be kind to you or have some empathy for you.

'The greatest trait in the world is kindness.'

In the United States, they celebrate entrepreneurism. If I'd done this in America and had a bad three or six months, *The Wall Street Journal* wouldn't kick me, they'd just leave me alone. Similarly, if I'd had a great six months, *The Wall Street Journal* would celebrate it. Americans celebrate entrepreneurial success and they never, in any way, turn on anyone who's had a go. Australians are meant to have a fair-go culture, but we don't. Once you get past that, you're fine.

If anything, this business has made our family tighter, but it's also reminded me that by having a profile, there are ramifications outside of myself. And that is my wife and children. I have no problem with the press playing the ball with me, but I don't want any part of my family brought into it.

BK: Now, when you talk about the investment strategy of the fund and the strategy of the business, how do you think about those two things?

CA: They're different. The strategy of the business is to export Australian superannuation. I'm going to export that to the best companies in the world and some Australian companies that do global business. There's a huge under-allocation of the best global stocks to Australians. Over the next 20 years, hopefully I will be the exporter. A bit like Andrew Forrest exporting iron ore.

We have this wonderful endowment called superannuation. It's our fourth biggest pool in the world but, arguably, the opportunities outside Australia are different. Not necessarily better, but different.

BK: More diverse.

CA: There are industries and sectors that are simply not represented, so the business strategy is to export Australian superannuation into a diverse range of the best companies in the world. The most enduring companies. That's what

I think the future looks like. There will always be a growth angle to that, probably a bit of a technology and platform angle. The greatest brands in the world in the next 20-25 years will be even bigger in an aspirational world with a growing population. Australia is still way under-allocated to international equities and probably international property. That will change generationally. People our age and younger...

BK: ... have a different worldview.

CA: And a completely different approach to their travel. Twenty years ago, you couldn't fly to Melbourne for less than $1000; everyone took the bus. Now, people fly overseas. The younger generation are very international, they are very worldly in all their activity, but their investment portfolios, their retirement savings, don't reflect that.

That will change generationally. Most of the 65- to 70-year-old age bracket controls most of the wealth in Australia but, through time, that will be handed down to the next generation, who will be much more diversified in their investments and much more international. My job is to deliver performance and then connect with that next generation of investor. That's not in any way anti-Australia positioning. There are absolutely valid reasons to get your income and franking credits out of Australia. My whole strategy has been Australia for income, international for growth.

'My whole strategy has been Australia for income, international for growth.'

If you're going to get growth in Australia, you generally need international companies because everything's about addressable market. How big is the addressable market for this product, or good or service, and can they find the biggest addressable market? The answer is there are 24 million people in Australia; 7.4 billion in the rest of the world. There are 4.6 billion in Asia alone, so Asia is where the next 20 years is. But for me, the strategy of the business is firstly all those companies that sell into Asia.

BK: The big US companies.

CA: Like a Louis Vuitton. He controls the greatest brands in the world and is one of the greatest investors, one of the greatest businessmen of all time. That's a large part of my portfolio because their addressable market is limitless; their pricing power is limitless; and their ability to continue to grow by acquisition and create new brands is limitless.

BK: So the structure, the strategy for the fund is really long-term, enduring family ownership.

CA: Yes.

BK: And for the fund, exporting Australian superannuation to the best, most diverse range of global businesses.

CA: Yes, the best companies in the world. The most enduring, the greatest brands in the world.

BK: Structure of the business? Owned by you and Ellie?

CA: Yes, and also Kerry Stokes. Kerry Stokes has 20 per cent of it. He came in, put a good investment in the fund, and investment in the business; he's been great. We were hovering around just under $100 million as a fund. Kerry came along and said he wanted a piece of the business and he could provide us with some of the working capital. We're now moving well past $100 million, but getting through that was a huge point for the business. It's psychological – once you're over $100 million, people can give you $1 million and be 1 per cent of your fund.

We don't need to be the biggest fund in the world, but Kerry was a great endorsement for the business. Kerry and Ryan Stokes have been absolutely excellent giving us support. Even if I'm having a weak performance period, they stay very strong to the cause.

The rest of it is owned by me, Ellie and staff. I don't see that changing very much; we're not looking to be listed, even though Magellan is a wonderful success.

BK: Platinum.

CA: I tend to think fund managers are better off private. If I'm listed, the pressure to raise assets under management (AUM) is constant. Whereas my key focus must be performance of the fund. You're either a fund manager or a manager of funds. They're two different things.

'You're either a fund manager or a manager of funds.
They're two different things.'

If you're listed, you've really got to keep growing under all circumstances, just keep getting more and more money. Obviously, we all know there's a crossover between how much money you've got and performance, so it's a bit of a contradiction.

BK: True. Maybe it's a stage of life thing.

CA: You're seeing it now: John Sevior is one of the great fund managers in Australian history, and he's done a deal with Hamish Douglass, who's a great distributor of product.

BK: Chris Smith has moved off.

CA: Correct. I think you'll see more transactions like that where a fund manager might decide they're not really a salesman. If someone could sell your product, and you can stay true to front-running money, that's more interesting.

But for us, we're three years into it and working our way through all of that. The most important thing is to be truly reliable, keep doing what you're doing and grind it out; it's a long game.

I'll say it again. You're either a fund manager or a manager of funds – that's the difference between being listed and unlisted.

BK: So if you could change one thing, what would you change?

CA: I would have done this earlier. I'm 45 now and should have done it in my mid-30s. I wish I'd done it five years earlier even, but I was probably caught up in meaningless stuff: thinking I'm a big shot with a big following in stockbroking; able to move a share price by what I wrote. Not operating in a humble and realistic world, which funds management is.

It's a true test every day. Even my stockbroking track record: you can't prove you're good or not; there's no track record. This is daily. Daily accountability with people's hard-earned cash. It's empirical evidence.

It's different to my stockbroking or investment strategy writing career. I wish I'd done it a bit earlier, but I also wish I'd been a bit more of a grown-up a bit earlier.

BK: Yes. It grows you up, the process.

CA: It does. Quite frankly, I'm a much better investor now from going through the process of building a small business. You understand cash flow, you understand balance sheets, you understand strategy, you understand time, you understand cost, you understand things pretty bloody well, pretty quickly.

Being a business owner makes you a better investor; there's no doubt about it.

'Being a business owner makes you a better investor; there's no doubt about it.'

The biggest thing in investing – and in life – is to look forward. The present is very effectively priced.

With high-frequency trading, there's Twitter, Facebook; everyone's got the same information at the same time. You can't make money out of the present. I'm not going to beat a high-frequency trader; someone who's invested $500 million in algorithms. Not me. But with time, conviction and duration, you will probably win. So you've always got to try and visualise the future, always have a portfolio that reflects the future.

I've got written on one of my screens: You never overtake anyone driving in the same lane. It doesn't mean we need to be in the outside lane, but if you're just mimicking everyone else, or you've got the same investments as everyone else, well, you probably won't do any better than them.

'You never overtake anyone driving in the same lane.'

BK: Yes, you see it so often when you're driving. If you stay in the lane and do the speed limit, the number of cars that come in and out, yet never seem to end up in front of you.

CA: That's high portfolio turnover. It's just chasing everything.

BK: Exactly. Consistency makes a huge difference.

CA: Consistency, transparency, and just being honest and accountable. We're dealing in a post-Hayne Royal Commission world where the opportunity for independent people who are honest and transparent and work hard is enormous. It's so important. The opportunities for all of us in the independent financial world are enormous.

'The opportunity for independent people who are honest and transparent and work hard is enormous.'

BK: It's massive.

CA: Some of the big brands that haven't behaved well at all, again, were driven by the needs of the share market for them to grow. The short-term needs of the share market.

BK: My sense is that it's more executive remuneration than the mindset of the market.

CA: Yes, I think that's probably right.

BK: Because the CEO comes in, writes everything off, prices up his options at the right number, but he's only there for three years so bang, bang, bang, he cashes out.

CA: That's right.

BK: Remuneration is a bigger issue than the market itself because the market is the investors. And most of the money is long-term super money that they're not looking to trade. So, what's going wrong with the management? Too many people investing money aren't putting enough pressure on the remuneration structures.

CA: There is also a mismatch in duration between the remuneration and when you get the reward for the capital allocation – or not. For me, it's really important that I'm accountable. There's a reason I put my name on the door. I'm accountable for the – good, bad, indifferent – performance.

BK: It's not business; it's personal.

CA: You can pick a Latin name and hide behind it or you can put your own name on the door and take the good and the bad. It was important to me to put my name on the door. It wasn't about empire building, it's not an egotistical thing. It's an accountability thing.

BK: Thank you very much.

INVESTMENT WISDOM LESSONS

• E is for effort

My business motto is ROE: return on effort.
Return of effort is measurable.

• Forward plan

The biggest thing in in investing – and in life – is to
look forward. The present is very effectively priced.

• Don't stay still

You never overtake anyone driving in the same lane.

Andrew Clifford

Co-founder, CEO and CIO of Platinum Asset Management

'I always knew I wanted to be in business.'

Andrew M. Clifford is the CEO, Executive Director and
Chief Investment Officer at Platinum Asset Management,
a Co-Manager at Platinum International Fund and a Portfolio
Manager at Platinum Asia Fund. He is on the Board of Directors
at Platinum Asset Management.
He co-founded Platinum in 1994 as the Deputy Chief Investment
Officer. Since taking over the role of Chief Investment Officer
in 2013, he has spent considerable time and effort improving
the organizational structure of the gradually expanding the
investment team to make the execution of the investment
process more seamless and efficient. With full endorsement from
the Board, he took over the role of CEO in 2018.
He worked for several years at Bankers Trust and perfecting the
craft of uncovering the overlooked gems in the stock market,
believing that irrational market sentiments and the consequential
short-term volatility can often lead to opportunity in companies
whose true worth is temporarily under-appreciated.
Andrew received his Bachelor of Commerce degree from
the University of New South Wales.
www.platinum.com.au

Interview

BRETT KELLY: If there was a motto, quote or thought that best summarised your approach to life, what would it be?

ANDREW CLIFFORD: In life, and particularly in the investing business, what is extraordinarily important is persistence. The world tends to value the great inspirational idea or thought, but they only come along as a result of a great deal of persistence. You just have to keep going. Investing is a very long-term game; it's like running a marathon except there's no finish line. I don't think life is too different to that.

BK: A marathon, not a sprint. So in terms of your upbringing, what is your background?

AC: I grew up in Sydney and have lived here all my life. My parents met late; my father was in the air force at the end of World War II. They were older for their generation, around 40 when they had me. I have a sister who is five years older than me; we lived a very quiet life on the North Shore.

Mum and Dad were both in the cosmetics industry. By the time I was in high school, they'd gone into business for themselves selling wholesale and retail-discounted cosmetics; they were the forerunner of companies like Priceline. They worked seven days a week, all day.

Of course, my sister and I were drawn into the business in our teenage years, and I did deliveries for them a day or two a week through my university days. I always knew I wanted to be in business.

BK: What did you study at university?

AC: I did an honours degree in commerce at the University of New South Wales; it was all accounting and finance. At school I was pretty much a slacker until around Year 10; I just did the minimum. Somewhere in those later years of school I worked out – I'm not quite sure why – that it was easier to just do the work, and then I actually quite enjoyed it. I can tend to become quite obsessed with things, so I worked extraordinarily hard in my final years of school.

I probably levelled out a little at university – I had learned how to study, and how to apply myself, so I did an honours year. I did a thesis on currency option pricing and had discussions with the head of the faculty about pursuing an academic career. At the time, I was quite interested in pursuing that, but I had a good offer to work for Kerr Neilson at Bankers Trust.

BK: What was your role at Bankers Trust?

AC: I was a trainee investment analyst. Back then, Bankers Trust had two funds management divisions. There was the larger one run by Olev Rahn, which had a top-down, macro-asset-allocation approach to investing. Then there was the one that Kerr Neilson had created to run the newly launched equity funds. I joined his team at the end of 1988. I was part of an interesting group of people: Paul Moore, Chris Selth and Rohan Hedley. Chris became my mentor, as well as Kerr. Everyone has gone on to do quite different things.

BK: What drew you to the role?

AC: In Year 10 commerce we went on an excursion to the stock exchange where we watched the chalkies put up bids and offers. I knew that was too frantic for my personality, but I was interested in the idea that you could buy parts of companies and I always wanted to do that. When I left university and was looking for a job, I wanted to get into equities, but no-one had that type of job – it didn't exist.

I remember Citigroup had just brought in a broker because it was in the early days of deregulation, but none of the banks were into brokering. I didn't want to get into brokering because it was a sales job – I wanted to understand companies and invest in them. I probably got the only job in the whole country where that was possible.

'I wanted to get into equities, but no-one had that type of job – it didn't exist.'

BK: Why was that?

AC: I remember saying to Kerr in the interview that the changes in media ownership laws had been discussed for a long time, and if you'd understood what that meant – in terms of the way these businesses worked – you would have been able to foresee the changes and take advantage of them, which is exactly the sort of thing we do. It was a very lucky answer – and probably the only thing of any value that I had to offer. Back then, students didn't think strategically about the interview process or getting hired. You just did lots of interviews and hoped someone gave you a job.

BK: Have there been any principles from your working relationship with Kerr or early career that have stayed with you?

AC: Absolutely. The core of what we do today is the same as what we were doing back then. It may have become more sophisticated, but essentially, it's the same: opportunities are to be found in those parts of the market that others are avoiding and those places where change is happening. It's about avoiding the crowd and looking in the neglected or unloved parts of the market.

'Opportunities are to be found in those parts of the market that others are avoiding and those places where change is happening.'

Today, we would talk in terms of cognitive biases, but it comes down to your intuitive response: you often know when your investing is wrong. To establish whether stocks are mispriced, you need to understand the whole business. The competitive advantage model of Porter's was fundamental to the way we looked at investing. What's the competitive environment? Who are the suppliers? The customers? What is the government and regulatory environment? That's the one that people always like to ignore. And we always look at the sustainability of the business – if a company is earning above-average returns on its capital, how long will that last?

So I learned that very basic framework; it was certainly Kerr's focus. It's all in our book, *Curious Investor Behaviour,* which has been in print for 15 years. Back then, behavioural finance didn't exist, but it certainly was the core. Kerr had been operating in that fashion for some time. There was also an absolute respect for the efficiency of the market. You can look at that in terms of the efficient market hypothesis, but I'd just talk in terms of: where do you have an understanding that's better than most? Insiders always have a better understanding.

'Insiders always have a better understanding.'

BK: I read about Kerr's seven observations in the *Australian Financial Review* recently, and he said that humility was very important. I think you're touching on that here in terms of respect for the market, respect for the insight and smarts of other people. But it also talks to your comment about persistence.

How have you inculcated this respect and, to a degree, humility in your team?

AC: Every individual needs to go through being taught a lesson by the market. Unfortunately, over time there have been people who were quite capable of being extraordinarily good investors, but you weren't able to impart that knowledge on to them. Ultimately, the lesson had to be taught by the market itself. In education, there's the concept of growth mindset. In this game, anyone with a fixed mindset is going to get...

BK: Eaten alive?

AC: Yes. As a team, you will go through periods of overconfidence, but when you've been through enough cycles you learn to level it out. There will always be a certain starting point in humility for the individual and for the team. That's when you start to learn.

'Every individual needs to go through being taught a lesson by the market.'

BK: What qualities do you think are essential for investment success?

AC: To be really good at this, you need to have a desire to understand how things work. That can be on a whole lot of different levels – from how a product is made, to how a system works, or how interest rates impact markets and growth. Otherwise, you'll just get washed along with the prevailing thoughts of the day.

Everyone is obsessed with levels of debt at the moment. You have to ask, how much is the right amount of debt? And what framework do you use to decide whether it's a lot or a little?

Again, you have to have a growth mindset, a natural inquisitiveness, and a desire to learn and understand. Why did this work? Why didn't that work? And there's got to be an appreciation that sometimes you make money even though you were wrong – and sometimes you lose money even though you were right.

In a place like this, the training is on the job and on the go. That's where persistence comes in again; the 10,000 hours required to gain expertise applies.

'You have to have a growth mindset, a natural inquisitiveness, and a desire to learn and understand.'

BK: How systematic are you in terms of documenting where you have and haven't made money, and interrogating the process that led to those results?

AC: We do look at it, but not as closely as we'd like. The thing you really need to do is document, as you go along, why you made your decision in the first place.

BK: Write the actual deal thesis upfront because people tend to rewrite history.

AC: Yes. And you remember things completely differently. I was doing an interview about the ten-year anniversary of the crash and I thought, 'I don't know how well I remember that'. So I got all of our quarterly portfolios out from that period and it's very different to what I remember. Being able to document things and review them later is a huge advantage in your learning. It's something we can do more of because that is how we'll develop our own capabilities much faster.

'Being able to document things and review them later is a huge advantage in your learning.'

BK: There is a lot of forward looking in business, but not so much retrospective analysis.

AC: The GFC is a good example. Pre-GFC, we went into that period with very little net investment position. We were down in the 50s, we had lots of shorts, and some very unusual longs. A lot of Japanese stocks. But in the end, everything went down. Clearly, there wasn't a great level of confidence in 2009 or 2010, and we weren't expecting that the world would come flying back as it did. Since then we've basically tracked the market, but we could have done a lot better if we'd been more reflective instead of just saying it's all over.

BK: Is the problem excess debt?

AC: I have a theory that it's not just about the level of debt; it's about capital. It could be debt or indeed equity – the issue comes when you get big accumulations of it in one sector of the economy. You will cause overinvestment, and then you will have some kind of unwinding.

'I have a theory that it's not just about the level of debt: it's about capital.'

It happens all the time. We had one in the oil patch in the United States in 2013. We also had it in China post-2012, and those ramifications are still working through that economy. So it can be in a country or in a sector, but basically, it happens where there's too much investment.

It may be refracted in secondary markets, like the traded equity and debt markets. Or it may not be. You may not be able to see it.

But, ultimately, there will be poor investment returns because of it. That might mean non-performing loans if you've been a lender. If you're an equity holder, it might mean bankruptcy or just very poor stock price performance. They're the outcomes.

What happened in 2008 was that those problems were so large and severe – because of the structure of the debt and because Lehman's was allowed to fail – that it broke the financial system. The interbank market broke down, the banks wouldn't lend to each other, and companies couldn't get money for the most basic needs.

That created a huge, much broader recession – and indeed problem – because the day-to-day occurrences, like leaving your house to go to work and use whatever capital that your company used to employ you to create economic activity, could no longer happen.

So, it wasn't because there was too much debt. It was because, all of a sudden, you couldn't get money for anything because the financial system was so damaged.

BK: It was too little trust, rather than too much debt.

AC: Yes. And you'll get that in the Asian crisis, and in Turkey today. We went through the oil patch blow-up in the US and there were bad debts and bankruptcies and markets took a breather for two or three months and then went on.

BK: Certainly Greece did.

AC: It was good for the rest of the economy that the oil price collapsed. In 2001 there was a bit of debt building up in the corporate sector in the US, but 2001 was about equity capital.

BK: Going too hard, too fast.

AC: Into technology.

BK: In one place.

AC: Then you had the unwinding of that. So the simplistic idea that there's too much debt is missing the point.

*'The simplistic idea that there's too much debt
is missing the point.'*

BK: It's more an allocation issue.

AC: Yes. And it's also about looking at the financial side of the economy. We all do that because it's what we can measure. It's one of our classic biases.

But the actual economy is not debt and equity and money markets. The economy is people going to work, the capital equipment of all types that they have access to, and the resources of the land. That's the economy, and they're a constant. It's a question of how well they've been employed year to year, but we don't talk about that because no-one measures them, and we don't know them.

So, you get more debt and less equity simply because interest rates are lower and we refinance the system. Is that a good thing, a bad thing? If you're the guy with a lot of debt and interest rates go up five per cent, it's going to be a bad thing. Both for the guy who lent you the money and for you.

BK: So, is this the confidence in the market, in the sort of respect for the efficiency of the market to say that the market will reallocate?

AC: It does work if it's allowed to work. There are plenty of examples in history when the state can impose and stop it working. That's certainly going on in the world today, so you can't be completely blind to those factors.

BK: Hence your comment about government and regulatory factors; one of Porter's forces that are often ignored.

AC: It can be, yes. It's a critical one. There's barely an industry where it hasn't happened. Look at our own finance industry. It's going to be a big part of it. That's why rules and regulations exist.

BK: Did you know that the Latin word for credit is credo, which means trust? The GFC was a breakdown of trust.

AC: Absolutely.

BK: When no-one trusts anyone, everything stops. If you look at Asia, or Africa, places where it's hard to invest and get a return, it's a value system – corruption means there is no trust in the system.

AC: Or there's less trust, yes.

BK: Then the real economy that you talk about just seems to operate more slowly.

AC: Yes, because without that recycling of savings from people who have them to those who can use them, the system doesn't work efficiently.

'Without that recycling of savings from people who have them to those who can use them, the system doesn't work efficiently.'

BK: So there's a real speed around trust.

AC: One of the interesting things is that even if you look at the growth rates of places like Pakistan, which is an economy in political upheaval, it's actually grown very well over the last two or so decades.

The changes as a result of the internet are also interesting. It's giving people information and an ability to transact. So if you're living in a rural village in India, you can now find the information to become a chicken farmer, purchase the things you need, and know where to sell your end product.

BK: And mobile bank in a way that you couldn't before. It's massive in Turkey.

AC: Yes. So it's really interesting how some technologies are actually evolving because you're not really replacing trust there, you're putting something else in place. If you think about mobile phones, they didn't take off in the emerging world until people came up with pre-paid.

BK: What do you feel your biggest mistakes have been?

AC: The investing mistakes are always the same; just in a different form. It's wanting the world to be the way you think it should be, rather than the way it actually is.

Not so much in the last three years, but over the last ten years, what I've seen a lot of is outrage about quantitative easing – how it was inappropriate policy and how it was going to ruin the world. That may be correct, but as an investor, the only question you have to ask is: what is the policy going to be? And what is that going to mean for the price of the assets that I'm investing in? Forget the rest of it. The thing is, we'll never know whether it was good policy or not because we'll never see what the alternative would have been.

Wanting to see the world the way you think it should be, rather than the way it is, is the classic investment – and probably business – mistake. You may have the greatest product, but you actually have to sell it.

'Wanting to see the world the way you think it should be, rather than the way it is, is the classic investment – and probably business – mistake.'

BK: You see that in start-ups.

AC: Yes, all the time in technology. I was covering tech in the 1998-2003 period, and so many companies theoretically had a great product, but it didn't matter because they were up against Microsoft and had to sell against them. It's subjective versus objective.

BK: How do you actually build an investment case as a team and sign it off?

AC: To start with, we don't sign it off as a team, that's the main thing. The individual analyst will have worked through the idea. We put a lot of focus on debate through the entire process.

BK: Who decides what you will look at?

AC: It can be an individual, so it could be Kerr, it could be me, it could be one of the analysts, or it could be our quant team. But once you're in the flow over a period of time, there's almost a natural consequence, to a degree, of how that unfolds. Sometimes it's hard to look back and know who thought of an idea, but there will have been someone who thought we should look at it, then there will have been basic research done on the company, the industry and so on. In a more formal sense, the case will be written up and there will be a debate around the table about it.

BK: The analyst writes the case up?

AC: Yes.

BK: And that goes up to a portfolio manager?

AC: Well, it goes to anyone who might wish to buy it. The sector team will have been debating the idea as it's worked through before everyone meets to discuss, but that is the formal process only. Often I might have been in the kitchen making a cup of tea while talking about it. Or you walk over to people's desks.

It comes back to the mistakes you make in investing, and probably in business as well: if you have seven people in a room talking about a particular investment

idea and everyone walks out thinking it's a great idea, that's a terrible idea. The good ideas should be uncomfortable. There should be something about them that's stopping you from doing it and you have to get past whatever that is.

'The good ideas should be uncomfortable.'

BK: So you're not seeking consensus?

AC: No. We remain constructive and the final decision rests with the portfolio manager. For any stock, there's going to be somewhere between four to six portfolio managers who might buy it and they will make their individual decisions. That's not to say that there's any cut-off point. We have what we call the stock meeting, but the debate goes on for days and weeks, and possibly years, after that fact.

BK: After you've bought it or not bought it.

AC: Yes. The interesting thing is when you get a situation where say, Kerr's buying the stock and I'm not. If we're theoretically both looking at the world in the same way, then why the discrepancy?

Working that out is the interesting part; working through those differences and discussing them. Sometimes you'll just have to agree to disagree.

BK: Obviously, as information changes, it is a continual discussion, it's not a fixed position; not a fixed mindset.

AC: Whatever the case today, in 18 months' time it can be completely different. The issues just keep changing.

BK: What role do you think you've played in the strategy of the business?

AC: We really did start with the simple idea that we thought we had an investment process that would deliver good outcomes for clients; that's what we were here to do. The other part of the ethos – and this is very much Kerr's thing – is that you have to understand that if someone's entrusted you with their savings, and you lose it, they don't get to earn that again. A retiree can lose half their nest egg because you managed it badly.

'It's a very serious responsibility when people trust you to look after their money.'

'It's a very serious responsibility when people trust you to look after their money. It means you don't try and maximise returns for people; you're not swinging for the fences.'

It's a very serious responsibility when people trust you to look after their money. It means you don't try and maximise returns for people; you're not swinging for the fences. For example, Samsung's an extraordinary investment opportunity today; I have three per cent in it. There are people who would say I should have a high conviction portfolio – have 15 per cent in it – but there are too many things in the world I don't know about. The funny thing is, in some portfolios a three-per cent position in Samsung would be underweight!

The final thing is: there was no plan B. Many people start an investment management business, they do well and get money in the door. But then they struggle to continue to do that, or they go through a period when they're not doing as good a job as they want, so they bring in a big sales force. That's when you start making acquisitions, branching out and doing all sorts of different things.

The thing is, now that you're doing all these other things to maintain your business, the risk is that you start to worry less about...

BK: Doing the business.

AC: Doing the business. The problem as a business – and for anyone who's a shareholder in a company with that mentality – is that it's quite possible that the other path is better in terms of building the business...

BK: From the head stock return.

AC: For us, if we can't do a good job for our clients, the business won't grow. In fact, it will shrink. That's the end outcome. But it also means that we actually need to focus on what we do. So that has been the core of what we do from day one, and still is. We have spent a lot of time in the last ten years thinking about how we can do parts of the business better. There's a huge level of trust in the organisation because of the improvements we've made to the client relationship. We've built out our investment specialists team, and there's been a lot of effort made to help people understand what we're doing. This is critical when the results aren't what they expect – in our view, if clients don't stick through the cycle, they don't get the benefit of what we do.

BK: Then you can't get the returns for them and they don't get them either.

AC: No-one wins in that situation. Instead, we've focussed on building access points. But the core of what we do hasn't changed.

BK: How hard has it been to maintain that?

AC: I have a pet theory that a dominant shareholder helps in terms of staying on strategy.

'A dominant shareholder helps in terms of staying on strategy.'

BK: A dominant shareholder does tend to deliver some level of focus, for a period anyway.

AC: That's probably right. The way this business is structured, even if the shareholders were different, it would be very difficult for them to do something else and maintain the integrity of who we are.

BK: So how is the business structured?

AC: If you go back to our beginnings, there was Kerr and three of us in a room. We built the team out from there. Starting around a decade ago, we had a team of 25 plus. You knew what 10 or 15 people were doing, but what were the rest doing?

We'd never actually worked out how you engage in this investment process as a group of people. It was all like, go find me this stock, and come back and tell me about it, and we'll have a discussion about it because we wanted to keep searching for ideas and having a debate. It's not a task-driven thing where you do your work on BHP, for example, and then put it aside. Ultimately, the idea was to get back to small teams within the greater team. That was a process that took a little while to refine.

If you look at management theory, it's pretty standard stuff that you can't have the head of the team having more than six to eight people reporting to them. So we had to get people to change the way they work, which they weren't used to. It was an interesting process.

All of a sudden, in a group of three or five people who are sitting down each week to discuss ideas, it became pretty apparent pretty quickly if someone didn't have anything to offer. Whereas before, it was possible to just occasionally say something and look fine. So there was a lot of pressure on the team to perform. It also made us focus on the need for people to work in a collaborative, collegial fashion.

We compete, but we compete with the market, not with each other. It became apparent that people were competing internally, and that takes time to move on from. We now have a very solid reincarnation of what we were.

'We compete, but we compete with the market, not with each other.'

BK: How many teams are there now? How many people?

AC: There are six teams.

BK: And total people?

AC: We've probably just moved through to 36 or so now. With Kerr stepping aside, the discussion around who would be the next CEO has been interesting: it had to be someone internal and it had to be an investment person because there weren't any decisions that were going to be made without the impact on the investment function being considered. Is it strong enough to do that? How's it going to be done? They're the key questions, not whether we're going to get a client, or what's it going to cost, or whatever. Because, how do those activities impact the core of the business, which is investing.

BK: Do you still run a team?

AC: I'm Chief Investment Officer and CEO, which is what Kerr was. I've been Chief Investment Officer since 2013, so I've been running the whole team formally since then. Sitting across the top of the teams. Kerr's now a member of the investment team. He remains on the board as a director, but he's not chairman.

Outside of the investment team, the organisation has two distinct functions: finance (legal, compliance and IT), which is run by our CFO. That is currently Andrew Stannard (who was the CFO of AllianceBernstein Asia Pacific), but our founding CFO was Malcolm Halstead. We run an extraordinarily efficient operation in that area. The other parts of the business are the client-facing parts (investor services, marketing). Liz Norman's run that since day one.

BK: And how many people are in each of those teams?

AC: The organisation's up over 100 now. It's probably going to be 25 under Liz and the rest under Andrew. Along the way we've seen other businesses start who have done well, but haven't really developed. Even today, the most popular way to start in this business is to go off to one of the incubators. They'll provide you with the admin, the sales team, put in some capital and take a stake in you. You don't have to worry about different things like compliance, regulation, accounting and auditing. But sometimes, it's in doing the difficult things that you actually grow muscles. I'd say they're giving away a huge amount for what they're getting. Compliance is problematic, but it's not impossible – and it will make you a better business.

We've always seen the main part of running this business as running the investment team and the CEO is the person organising, managing the investment team.

BK: That's the big gig.

AC: It is. On day one there were four of us running money. Somewhere along the line someone started thinking about how we organise things and sort them out. By 2013 I was already that person.

I was running money as well, but Kerr was very focused on the selling and marketing of the business. I was worried about getting the group organised so they could be as productive as possible. It was a natural progression.

The biggest transition is that Kerr has completely stopped managing money. That happened as of 30 June. I'd been running global money since 2011, but I've run money in Asia since my second year of working with Kerr.

We've been working together for 30 years; I've been running money for 29. I spent some time running our tech fund during the excitement in the US, but Asia's been my speciality. I was investing in companies in China before there was a stock market there.

'I was investing in companies in China before there was a stock market there.'

Kerr's stepped back from managing global money and those portfolios have been reassigned to me and Clay Smolinski, who's also been running money for a decade, mainly in Europe. He's been running global funds for five years now. That's the most fundamental change, but it's a progression. We've been working toward it for a long time. I handed the Asia fund over to Joseph Lai over what was probably a five-year period.

We've been through this in Europe when Toby Harrop, who was one of our founders, retired. Clay took that over and then he progressed that to Nik Dvornak. The Japan fund has been through four portfolio managers in its history.

You begin to realise that there's a safety net here – every portfolio manager who's been here – 14 in total – every one of them has had a record of good performance. Even when a new portfolio manager joins a fund, every stock there has been covered; it has been thought about by a number of portfolio managers.

BK: For a long time.

AC: Yes, so when you come into a particular portfolio, a third of the stocks might be yours. It's not like all of a sudden I'm running $12 billion instead of six. It's a steady progression that we have been working on across the board since 2011. To me, that's the big change.

If you look at those two functional areas through time, I've been on the management committee from day one. I'm familiar with the issues and the people, and I'm taking over a very able team.

BK: So how are you managing the succession?

AC: Kerr's still a full-time employee on the investment team. He's spending his time on investment ideas and he's debating them enthusiastically with the analysts and portfolio managers. It's all part of the environment; it's what we've always done. The portfolio managers have been making decisions independently of Kerr for quite some time. We all know how to engage in debate and discussion.

BK: Is the board genuinely independent?

AC: We've been through a period of board renewal. As a listed company, we've just gone through ten years and we've had new members come on the board over the last three. They're all strong, independent voices. They are very impressive in terms of their achievements and background. We do have two shareholders who have 50 per cent of the business.

BK: To change tack, in terms of life and family, how do you manage the size role you have and life more broadly?

AC: There's no magic formula. I met my wife Jane at university: we've been married since I was 23. I'm 52 now. We've got two kids; it's a very busy household. You just get up in the morning and keep moving with whatever's going on.

BK: Persistence.

AC: Maybe! Whether it's dropping the kids to school, which I don't have to do anymore, or taking them to sporting events – I think we've just had our last game of school netball ever – you just get up and you do whatever's in front of you and you keep going! You can always wonder if you could have used your time better, but there hasn't been a lot of time spent sitting around doing nothing!

BK: One final question: if you could change one thing what would you change?

AC: We started this as a group of people who understood investing. We managed money really well, but may not have managed people particularly well. If I'd understood in my mid-20s that you actually do need to manage people, and had learned those skills, I would have been a lot further ahead.

BK: Excellent, we'll finish there. Thank you.

INVESTMENT WISDOM LESSONS

• Persist

In life, and particular in the investing business, what is extraordinarily important in persistence.

• Trust your gut

It comes down to your intuitive response: you often know when your investing is wrong.

• Look back to look forward

Being able to document things and review them after is a huge advantage in your learning.

Bill Ferris

Co-Chairman, Castle Harlan Australian
Mezzanine Partners (CHAMP)

*'In giving is
receiving.'*

Bill has been Co-Chairman of CHAMP's Investment Committee since 2014. Previously, he was the Executive Chairman of CHAMP, a role he held since its formation in 2000, and of its predecessor Australian Mezzanine Investments Ltd (AMIL), which he co-founded in 1987 with Joe Skrzynski.

A veteran of private equity in Australasia, Bill founded Australia's first venture capital firm, International Venture Corporation, in 1970. He was made an Officer of the Order of Australia in 1990 for services to the export industry and, in 2008, was made Companion in the Order of Australia for his philanthropic activities.

Awards honouring Bill's contribution to the private equity sector include Private Equity International 2013 Leader of the Year Asia-Pacific; the Asian Venture Capital Journal Lifetime Achievement Award in 2008; and an Australian Private Equity and Venture Capital Association Limited (AVCAL) Lifetime Contribution Award in 2008.

Bill holds a The Bachelor of Economics (Honours) from the University of Sydney and a Master of Business Administration (MBA) from Harvard Business School where he graduated as a Baker Scholar in 1970. He was the inaugural Chair of the Innovation and Science Australia Board (2016-2018) and a member of the Harvard Business School Asia Pacific Advisory Council (2008-2018).

https://cpecapital.com

Interview

BRETT KELLY: Bill, I wanted to start with a question: if there was a motto, quote or thought that best summarises your approach to life, what would it be?
BILL FERRIS: I'd have to go with the old Franciscan tenet: in giving is receiving. In my experience, whether it's giving of your time, your help, your money, your mindfulness – you feel better for it, and you are better for it.

By bringing out the best in other people, you will bring out the best in yourself. That's not to say that I've been overly successful in doing that, but I'm aware when I am doing it – and I'm now very aware when I'm not doing it.

'By bringing out the best in other people,
you will bring out the best in yourself.'

BK: So, let's talk about the business, CHAMP Private Equity. It was built as a partnership between yourself and Joe Skrzynski. *(See page 174 for an interview with Joe Skrzynski.)*

BF: Yes, Joe and I have worked together in the business for 30 years. We look at a deal and I'm in the why-not camp and Joe will be in the what-if camp; it's worked really well for us.

BK: How did you get started?

BF: My first start-up was at age 25; it was a very small venture capital company I initiated when I came out of the Harvard Business School in Boston. I'd already spent about nine years in the workforce at the great imperial Colonial Sugar Refining (CSR) Company, as it was called. Women weren't allowed to smoke and almost not allowed to talk. It was a long time ago culturally; a lot of things have since changed.

I started in the mail room at 16, which was fantastically interesting because once you had sorted the mail into pigeon-holes, you physically took the mail around to the different divisions and executives. It was amazing what you got to see and hear – and puzzle about. I was lucky to be moved into the accounting department and then the data processing division. This included a mainframe computer and punch card team which occupied an entire subterranean floor of CSR's high-rise head office. I learned a little coding and was fascinated by what was happening in the very early days of information technology. I learned a lot early on from a big business like CSR.

I was also fortunate to be the assistant to Bryan Kelman, who eventually rose to be CEO of CSR. At the time, he had come back from the UK to run CSR's ready-mix concrete acquisition. He was chairman or director of a number of operating boards and would throw me in at the deep end as his alternate. As a result of his mentorship – in particular with the concrete and quarrying industry and other assets the company held at the time – I gained wonderful exposure to capex decision making and people management.

'As a result of Bryan Kelman's mentorship – in particular with the concrete and quarrying industry and other assets the company held at the time – I gained wonderful exposure.'

BK: What made you decide to study at Harvard? It would have been quite a new school in the early 1960s.

BF: I had completed my economics degree at the University of Sydney part time – working at CSR during the day and attending university at night. Then I did an honours degree; CSR gave me time off to make that possible.

In that time, I got to know Professor Jeremy Davis. He ultimately ran the Australian Graduate School of Management (AGSM), but at the time had just come back from Stanford where he did his doctorate. I told Jeremy I was interested in going to business school, and of course he suggested Stanford. I researched Stanford very closely, but Harvard was the holy grail for me – it was the best in terms of the social sciences; it was the crème de la crème and still is in my view. So Jeremy, who really encouraged me to think about studying overseas, and Bryan Kelman and CSR were extremely supportive. It was a very exciting time for me.

BK: How did you pay for your studies?

BF: It was very expensive, even then. I was fortunate to get a couple of scholarships, including the Denison Miller Scholarship from the University of Sydney. I also had a Fulbright Scholarship that helped, which CSR matched. That enabled me to go with some basic income. I had also been punting on the stock exchange, companies like Silver Valley (mining stocks), so I had built up a small amount of spending money, which meant I could buy a convertible Mustang when I hit Boston. I was all set.

BK: What did you gain from your time in Boston?

BF: The real benefit for me was being able to mix with an incredible milieu of people from all over the world. The amazing depth and variety of people's backgrounds – and how smart they all were – was very inspiring.

I was also amazed at how many Australians were at Harvard in all different faculties, not just the business school. This led to me starting what's now called the Harvard Club of Australia. We had an initial membership of 20 to 30 students, and it is still a very active club. Boston itself is an academic city, but it's also a very successful business community so it had a lot going for it. In 1968 to 1970, which is when I was there, venture capital had only just taken off in the capital markets; it was a very interesting time. To its credit, Harvard Business School had already incorporated new enterprise courses and modules into the business case study program, which they pioneered.

'In 1968-70, which is when I was at the Harvard Business School in Boston, venture capital had only just taken off in the capital markets; it was a very interesting time.'

These changes meant that you could be sitting in class with a professor and the actual start-up guys would be up the back. You'd be given a case study on why their business would or wouldn't work, and you would have to comment on what you would have done differently to accelerate it, for example. Would you put more of your own money into this company?

We were interacting with the actual founders and their business; it was real time stuff. I loved that. Your mettle was tested every day. It was very exciting, and my introduction to venture capital. It was then that the lightbulb went off for me.

BK: You decided that venture capital was something you'd like to do?

BF: Yes.

BK: Did you stay in the US after Harvard?

BF: Not for long. There was an Australian professor who was on the Harvard Business School faculty called David Hawkins. For the thesis requirement in

my second year, I wrote the case for a venture capital company to be started in Australia. I needed a professor to sponsor my work, so I asked David. In the end, I wrote it in the form of an information memorandum to start Australia's first venture capital company. That became my first start-up.

BK: Do you still have that document?

BF: I've got scraps of it; Harvard would have it. It was a good document because it was a why not document. I was making the case that Australia could be more than just a very successful quarry, which is how my American business school mates viewed Australia at the time. They didn't understand that we could do many other entrepreneurial and innovative things. It was a time in Australia when banks would never do a deal based on cash flow; they only ever banked bricks and mortar back then.

'I was making the case that Australia could be more than just a very successful quarry, which is how my American business school mates viewed Australia at the time.'

Frankly, I totally underestimated the challenges, but I was so excited about the opportunity. I've always been interested in starting things; start-ups. I was premature, in a sense, but it worked in the end.

BK: But you were first to market, which is so important.

BF: Yes. Like many students coming out of business school, I had the opportunity to work for venture capital companies in America, which was very enticing, but I thought if I didn't come back and follow through on my idea, I never would. That was what compelled me to return: I didn't want to miss an opportunity. I wanted to be the first to give it a go. That can be a powerful and compelling force to get on with things. In retrospect, I got a bit ahead of myself – I let the excitement trump the risks.

'I didn't want to miss an opportunity. In retrospect, I got a bit ahead of myself – I let the excitement trump the risks.'

BK: So, you're 25. You're back in Australia and you start the business.

BF: Yes, I started it in August 1970.

BK: You weren't married, and you didn't have any children, so in a sense, there wasn't any great risk?

BF: That's true; if it didn't work, I would have just gone on to the next thing, but I was confident enough to go for it.

BK: Take us through that.

BF: I mentioned the Australian Club at Harvard; I used to use the club letterhead to invite visiting ambassadors or senior business people who were interested in Australia to visit us on campus.

One of these people was a very interesting businessman and philanthropist called David Stone, who had a venture capital company in Boston, among other things. He also had agricultural interests in Australia, so I invited him to speak to the club and we became friends.

Two things arose out of that friendship that have been life changing. The first was that he encouraged me to give venture capital a go. He said that if we could get 50/50 funding – in Australia and America – I could count him in for underwriting the US half. That was a huge step.

BK: He agreed to match whatever you could raise in Australia?

BF: Yes.

BK: Massive. What was the amount you were trying to raise?

BF: I started off wanting to get about $750,000 total starting capital, but we finished up with $500,000. David put in half of that.

BK: That was a lot of money for the time.

BF: Today you wouldn't open the office, but back then it was a start. The second life-changing impact David had on my life was he kept saying I had to meet his niece out on the West Coast. About three years later, I did. To cut a long story short, Lea became my wife, trusted consigliore and mother of our three amazing children. We've been living in Sydney ever since.

BK: All because you invited him to speak at Harvard.

BF: That's where it started, yes.

BK: You've got this project, you raise your $500,000 and you're in Sydney. What was the initial focus?

BF: It was early stage and small business focused; the amount of capital we had was modest. I was of the view, however, that it was enough to get a small portfolio going. I thought we'd be able to leverage up banking sector support as well. We weren't going to go into capital-intensive mining operations, nor were we going into real estate, which was always well looked after by the property developers and the banks. We were looking for entrepreneurs needing cash for new ideas, building their businesses, expanding across a range of sectors. We were always conscious of technology impact.

'We were looking for entrepreneurs needing cash for new ideas, building their businesses, expanding across a range of sectors. We were always conscious of technology impact.'

In fact, it's interesting to think, 40 years later, one of the deals we did was a pioneering, off-peak, energy storage business selling to domestic consumers.

BK: How did that go?

BF: We lost the lot. I think we put in about $100,000.

BK: So, 20 per cent of your fund.

BF: Probably, yes. The concept was good; the product worked. Reasonable demand. But I underestimated the banks' risk aversion. It didn't seem like a lot of money at the time, but the banks lost patience with missed budgets and the company went into receivership. Basically, the company ran out of cash and management capability to meet their business plan – there were a lot of learnings in it for me.

BK: What cemented the reputation of your business and allowed you to really move forward?

BF: We had a company called Barlow Marine, which was a very innovative manufacturer of boat fittings, mainly sailing boat winches. It was a manufacturing company with a machine shop, a forging shop, a foundry – all that manufacturing intensity – but it had got into difficulties with management.

I went in to run the business as CEO, partly with the fund investment and some of my personal money. After a number of years, we turned it around, acquiring a small competitor in the UK, and then our largest competitor in the US. It became a small but global business, firstly via export success and then by the scale of market penetration by other acquisitions.

BK: Then what happened in terms of the impact?

BF: The company was well known; we'd won an export award, which also raised its profile and assisted our successful exit. By that time, we had also expanded our initial $500,000 capital and had a couple of million come in from Hill Samuel Australia, which is now Macquarie Bank. David Clark, who was the early CEO of Macquarie was on our board, as was Bryan Kelman. We had a really hot team, which was very helpful.

BK: How big do you think the fund was at that point?

BF: We never got much bigger than maybe $3 million.

BK: How did you scale up?

BF: Based on the success we had demonstrated with Barlow Marine and other small businesses, and given the gaping absence of any institutional VC or expansion capital, I thought it must be possible to attract some of the big super funds to give it a go. Surely it was time! So I approached Joe Skrzynski to gauge his interest. I'd known him from university days, and since graduating he had been very successfully involved in some private market transactions on behalf of Sir Paul Strasser.

'I thought we could start the first private capital business in the country backed by super funds, so I approached Joe Skrzynski to gauge his interest.'

We started a company in 1987 called Australian Mezzanine Investments Limited (AMIL). It was a management company for the first institutionally subscribed fund for private equity investing. We raised $30 million from four superannuation funds. At the time, the corporate super funds were very important. We gained support from Shell, BHP, State Super and CRA; there were commitments from five in total. We told them we thought the stock market was overvalued, but it was a

good time regardless. Indeed, if the market crashed, it might be an even better time for us. We got all the commitments; then the crash came.

So we went back to all five to discuss the way forward. The four I mentioned all reconfirmed and agreed that the buying opportunities for PE were even better now, but the other one pulled out. I must say, we were worried they would all pull out. After the stock market crash was a good time for value. It helped us, rather than hindered us.

With that first fund we were able to demonstrate that you can make money out of private equity. Of course, until very recently, the super funds in Australia adopted a very risk averse position to venture capital and PE.

BK: Still are.

BF: Yes. One of the great things to come out of this whole experience has been that we've now got superannuation funds back in to local venture capital funds – like Medical Research Commercialisation Fund, AirTree, Blackbird, Square Peg. It's fantastic; serious and patient money.

As soon as this fund showed that you could actually make very good returns, they started piling into private equity. They can't get enough of it now. It's been rewarding to see that happen because we kick-started the venture capital concept and then pioneered the private equity entry in Australia.

'We kick-started the venture capital concept and then we pioneered the private equity entry into Australia.'

BK: That's the theme I'm picking up. You're first into venture capital, you're first into this institutionally subscribed private equity market. Is it a ten-year fund?

BF: Yes, a ten-year fund.

BK: A ten year, close-ended, two-in-twenty type traditional fund?

BF: Yes, exactly. And then we did three funds in the name of Australian Mezzanine. Then with our colleague Su-Ming Wong we did a venture capital fund called AMWIN which was incredibly successful; we were in a number of internet start-up companies early on. One was LookSmart which did an initial public offering on the Nasdaq back in 1998, six months before the crash in 1999.

BK: Okay, that's 1999.

BF: Yes. We came out of escrow and sold four to five weeks before the tech crash of 1999. In that deal, we made over a hundred times our money for our investors.

At about $1.5 billion, it was then the highest valued tech stock ever from Australia. Sometimes, timing can trump analysis.

'Sometimes, timing can trump analysis.'

I've been asked if that was just good luck or smart decision-making, but in truth, we couldn't fathom the Nasdaq valuations. At that time, it was all about multiples of eyeballs. We rode with it, but we didn't want to be greedy, so we moved out.

BK: You've got to the year 2000, you've done five or six funds, and you're 55.

BF: Yes. We decided to step up the scale. All of our Australian Mezzanine funds were doing buy-outs, but also continuing with business expansion and venture capital deals. It was time to start a larger scale, dedicated buy-out firm with overseas investors. We were the first to bring offshore investors into Australian private equity. We did that by teaming up with a US venture firm called Castle Harlan in 1999 which assisted our access to some of the superannuation funds over there. Then it was a $500 million fund, pretty much 50/50 Australian/American; back to the old formula.

An influential US investor at that time, Harborvest in Boston and Hong Kong, was run by a Harvard Business School classmate... their decision to invest broke the ice for other US pension funds to also seriously consider Australia. Our first fund did really well; it sparked a whole lot of follow-on activity that we've seen to this day in the sector.

BK: When does CHAMP – Castle Harlan Australian Mezzanine Partners – become CHAMP?

BF: We became CHAMP pretty much from the get go.

BK: So that first fund, was that the first CHAMP fund?

BF: Yes. We leveraged the experience and infrastructure of both Australian Mezzanine and Castle Harlan.

BK: How much did Castle Harlan own?

BF: It was a 50/50 management company structure. After CHAMP 1 in 2000, we did CHAMP 2 in 2005, then CHAMP 3 in 2010. Castle Harlan's interest was bought out prior to CHAMP 4 today. We were keen to keep the CHAMP name going and stay involved longer, which meant getting a proper succession in place.

We really started on this transition pretty early, at least eight years ago, before we started CHAMP 3. We didn't want to go the way we'd seen lots of private equity and venture capital companies go – not succeeding with their succession plans; with founders who couldn't let go, or who didn't want to transition; selling up or failing.

We tried a few things and, to cut a long story short, John Haddock stepped up as CEO. He has made a success out of all of this. We recruited him a long time ago from one of the investment banks; he's been in the family for a long time. He's a very action-oriented guy, building the business and running CHAMP 4 very successfully. Joe and I agreed to play a grey-haired consigliere role as part of the ongoing story and stability for CHAMP – to give some comfort to investors – but really, it's the new team under John who's got the reins and are making the running.

Joe and I are investors in the fund; and we co-chair the investment committee. We get involved in the new deals and exits of old deals more than anything else now. So, fingers crossed, we're seeing CHAMP expand and succeed. CHAMP will probably launch fund number five before the end of 2019.

'Fingers crossed, we're seeing CHAMP expand and succeed.'

BK: What have been your learnings about succession from your experience?

BF: We wouldn't have started it any earlier, and ultimately, you've got to be careful that you don't put your own recipe into other people's cake-making. As leaders of the partnership, we've tried to be inclusive.

Over a long period of time, you build up habits and a culture, so it's a work in progress as to how John builds on that with his culture and style. We've done what we can, as carefully as we can, but time will tell. In terms of investment performance, investors want one thing now: cash on cash returns. John and his new team are going to deliver that.

'In terms of investment performance, investors want one thing now: cash on cash returns. John and his new team are going to deliver that.'

BK: What has helped you keep your goals so successfully?

BF: A couple of things. I am obviously passionate about start-ups. Trying to make a difference has been really important too. I like to think that I look for the best in people and I enjoy doing that. Even in this great era of disruptive technology and everything else – having great people is still where the rubber really hits the road. For me, anyway. I've been really fortunate with the people side of things.

Being able to team up with Joe Skrzynski has been tremendous. It's not that often that you can have a 30-year business partnership. As Joe says, we spend more time together than with our wives. We've had to deal with a lot of things together. We are more than just business partners, we are very close personal friends.

Really early on, right when we started, we were both interested in public policy; public good, and philanthropy. Whether that's money, time or volunteering, we both wanted to be involved in that, individually, so we decided to each allocate half a day a week to those activities. It's now grown to several days per week, so we have definitely grown outside interests.

Early on, I was involved in setting up Austrade. More recently, the healthcare area has been a focus for me, especially my 12 years as chair of the Garvan Institute of Medical Research. More recently I have enjoyed my time as chair of Innovation and Science Australia. Joe has been very involved with the film industry, and still is, and with Human Rights Watch on whose global board he now serves. We've tried pretty hard and will continue to do so.

BK: Has that commitment to external interests made you a broader and better investor?

BF: It's definitely made us broader. We've both learned that what goes around comes around, so it's not exactly a sacrifice. We enjoy being able to make a difference in these areas, but opportunities also come through those different networks and different people. For me, one of the things that my family foundation has backed is fellowships to Harvard Business School, in partnership with the Harvard Club of Australia, we send CEOs from not-for-profit organisations in Australia to the Harvard Business School's strategy course for NFPs. The Foundation has funded more than 40 so far, and the multiplier effect for these CEOs has been massive. It's gratifying for me and my family to be able to do this.

BK: Innovation and Science Australia is a huge passion of yours. What is the vision?

BF: When Prime Minister Malcolm Turnbull announced the National Innovation and Science Agenda at the end of 2015, he was very spirited about the need for innovation to shore up the Australian economy, reducing our dependency on our efficient resources sectors and to take on the emerging digital economy.

I accepted his invitation to chair Innovation and Science Australia, which is a statutory body that provides advocacy and independent advice to government on lifting Australia's innovation performance.

We rank very low in the OECD indexes to do with innovation and commercialisation of breakthrough research. It's not that we're bereft – we perform exceptionally well in the health and medical research area for example – but we were asked to create a strategic plan that would get Australia into the top tier of innovation nations by 2030.

We completed that work over a two-year period and have made our recommendations. The response from the government was good, but not enough. They responded to our recommendations about national missions for genomics and for the Great Barrier Reef, and a number of other things with quite bold responses and initiatives. For example, we pushed for a review of the Australian public service because we'd concentrated on what government can do in terms of innovative procurement, service delivery, data access and curation. Prior to the spill, Prime Minister Turnbull announced that review and it's now under way; Importantly the senior heads of department, the secretaries of the major agencies, the departments, are supporting this review.

BK: What has been the greatest lesson that you would like to pass on to your kids or grandkids?

BF: I would certainly say: pursue what you really enjoy and don't give up. It's good to dream a bit too. Just go for it.

'Pursue what you really enjoy and don't give up.
It's good to dream a bit too.'

I don't think you want to set yourself up for failure, but I do think you need to aim high – I often found that I didn't set the bar high enough. We've got such opportunity and privilege in this country; aim a bit higher and you'll make a difference. Whether that's to one person, or several, or a nation; it will be worth it.

BK: Thank you so much, Bill.

INVESTMENT WISDOM LESSONS

• Accentuate the positive
By bringing out the best in the other people, you will bring out the best in yourself.

• Be tenacious
Pursue what you really enjoy and don't give up.

• Be brave
Just go for it.

Jun Bei Liu

Portfolio Manager, Tribeca Investment Partners

*'Everywhere you
go in Australia
you feel a limitless
possibility.'*

Jun Bei has over 18 years of investment experience, the last 14 of which have been with Tribeca. Initially joining Tribeca in 2005 as an analyst covering consumer discretionary, staple, healthcare and REIT sectors, she was promoted to Deputy Portfolio Manager of the Alpha Plus Fund in 2016 and subsequently took over management of the fund in 2019. During her tenure, Jun Bei has covered most sectors across the Australian market at various times. As a native Chinese speaker Jun Bei has also brought unique macro and fundamental perspectives to Tribeca's investment process.

Prior to Tribeca, Jun Bei spent four years as a fundamental analyst covering the Australian consumer sectors at Morningstar and Foster Stockbroking. Jun Bei holds a Bachelor of Commerce (Finance & Economics) from the University of New South Wales. She is also a CFA charter holder and a member of the Australian Institute of Company Directors.

https://tribecaip.com/team/jun-bei-liu/

Interview

BRETT KELLY: Jun Bei, is there a motto, or a quote or thought that best summarises your approach to life?

JUN BEI LIU: This is probably true for life as well as investing: take the path less travelled. Good investments, where you generate significant returns, generally stem from decisions made when you go against the mainstream; where you took calculated risk; where you did your homework. These decisions can pay off quite handsomely.

In life, it's the same. Often people will just go with the majority: you do what you are taught to do; obey the rules; and keep to the path. It is a herd mentality. But if you don't panic, and aren't afraid to be bold, with hard work and a determination to be yourself, you will shine; you can find that path less travelled. You will achieve what you always wanted.

And have fun – that's incredibly important.

'If you aren't afraid to be bold, with hard work and a determination to be yourself, you will shine; you can find that path less travelled. You will achieve what you always wanted.'

BK: Excellent. Let me ask you about your background. How did you end up where you are today?

JBL: I was born in Shanghai, China, and only came to Australia when I was 16. Because of the one child policy, I'm a single child.

The China I grew up in is very different from the China today with all its shiny and modern buildings, especially in the big cities. In the 1980s, China had a closed border. Most Chinese families had only modest means and we had almost no access to anything foreign.

The transition from the early 1990s – from a closed China to opening the borders – was a time of expanding possibility. We then had access to foreign goods, films and technology; it was just incredible, so exciting to see such rapid change. The transition continued for me when I came to Australia in the mid-1990s. The first computer I touched was in Australia, an Apple. I still remember seeing the tiny apple when you turned it on. The changes from early 2000 until now – phones, tablets, just the access – it's incredible.

BK: So why did you leave China for Australia?

JBL: My mother came to Australia in the 1990s on a student visa, just after the Tiananmen Square protests. She came to build a home here, studying part time and working many jobs. In time she received permanent residency, but it meant she lived away from us for almost five years.

I remember when she came to China, she asked me if I wanted to stay in China, on the known path, the one that everyone follows. Essentially, I would finish school, do further study, work, marry, have kids, all of that. Or I could go to Australia, which was unknown. We didn't know what I would do – there were so many possibilities.

It wasn't much of a decision. I said yes to Australia because I felt it would lay a path that would be full of opportunities. The unknown was exciting; there were so many things that I could do. So I came with my dad to Sydney and we lived in Warriewood to start with, on the Northern Beaches.

'I said yes to Australia because I felt it would lay a path that would be full of opportunities. The unknown was exciting.'

BK: Very different to China.

JBL: That's right. Very quiet, very relaxing – that was my first impression. It was so beautiful and pristine too; Warriewood has one of the most amazing beaches. Very small but has beautiful cliffs.

In China, you don't see that much because it is so full of people. China has a phrase – people mountain, people sea – which I always thought was very accurate because when you look in front of you, it's just full of heads.

One thing I find in Australia is that everywhere you go, you feel a limitless possibility. You feel very encouraged in everything you do. My high school teacher would always say, you can do whatever you would like to do. Your ambition is only limited by your imagination.

'Your ambition is only limited by your imagination.'

It is quite different from the education system I went through in China, which is very prescriptive – this is what you should do, these are the formulas, memorise it; that type of education system. No encouragement to think outside the box.

BK: Where did you go to university?

JBL: I did a Bachelor of Commerce with a major in Finance at the University of New South Wales. Throughout school, being the Chinese kid, my mathematics was strong. Obviously, my English was a little lacking, but I did pick biology and a few other things because I found them interesting. The natural progression from a strong mathematics background is into a finance degree.

I spent a fair bit of time looking at behavioural finance and economics, as well as macro-economics, which I found fascinating. It's interesting to understand how minor changes in incentive can effect changes in how people behave.

While I was studying I worked part time with Aspect Huntley on Ian Huntley's old newsletter Your Money Weekly, and the Smaller Companies Guide. Essentially, they wrote stock recommendations for retail investors. I was fortunate to be part of that group in the early 2000s. As a university student, it was great to get an insight into real companies.

We learned about financial statements at university, but the practical side, the application is limited. Having the chance to look at real companies was fascinating. Every day we analysed and wrote about companies. Most exciting was actually going to visit the companies and having the chance to meet and interview management. Piecing together information from different sources, putting it together, working out what the market's looking for, whether a company is a buy or a sell; it's like a puzzle.

BK: So you finished your degree and went straight into full-time work at Aspect Huntley?

JBL: That's right, I worked as an analyst for two years. Toward the end of my time at Aspect Huntley, I took on the Chartered Financial Analyst (CFA) certificate, which gave me a global view of analysing companies. I learnt to analyse companies from multiple perspectives with support from knowledgeable professionals, I learnt from their experience and wisdom. Aspect Huntley has now been bought out by Morningstar.

After that I moved on to Foster Stockbroking, a small Sydney-based stockbroker. The owner Stuart Foster says he loved my energy and always saw my huge potential in covering stocks. That's when I moved from a junior to senior analyst. I gained experience and insight into technology in the consumer sector; media was a big sector back then as well. I also had a lot of exposure in terms of deal flow, structuring rights issues and building client relationships, mainly

with the companies. I came to understand the value of doing site tours and speaking with competitors; all important when attempting to gain an in-depth understanding of a company; it was really interesting.

BK: How long were you a senior analyst at Foster?

JBL: I was there for about 18 months before moving to Tribeca, which was called Jenkins Investment Management then. I was headhunted and asked to become part of that team, again covering more consumer-focused sectors as well as technology and the media space. I've been here since 2005.

BK: How have you progressed within the business?

JBL: The last seven years have been the most rapid transition of my career especially in the last 12 months, moving from an analyst to Deputy Portfolio Manager and the to the Lead Portfolio Manager role. Over the last seven years I have learnt to move from focusing purely on the fundamentals of an investment to building my understanding of portfolio construction. This is crucial part of delivering consistent returns to my investors.

I run the Tribeca Alpha Plus fund, it is a long short fund, with very active positions in companies seeking to take advantage of both rising and falling prices. The current market has provided many opportunities to test the full potential of this strategy.

BK: Is it global?

JBL: No, it's domestic. It a long short fund focus on the ASX 200 stocks. We look to consistently outperform our ASX benchmark by at least 5 per cent.

BK: What is the structure of the business?

JBL: There are about 26 people in the office. It was founded by David Aylward in the late 1990s. We've recently gone through an ownership transition and now staff owns 100 per cent of the business, Grant Samuel previously had a 49 per cent stake in our business.

BK: So what role has self-learning, versus formal training, played in your career?

JBL: Self-learning, and experience, are incredibly important. Real world experience fleshes out everything. This is often when real understanding in and insight are gained. Formal training provides a framework that you can build upon; it's like the skeleton, the bones. You can be taught how to look at things but until you experience it personally it's just theory.

In formal training, they'll teach you how to analyse a company, but to contextualise that, you've got to actually talk to the people involved and affected to really understand the opportunity. For example, forecasting earnings growth is crucial to investment but it requires insight. History is not always a good guide. How do you work out if it's a 5 per cent or 15 per cent growth rate and is management being reasonable in the guidance they are providing? It comes from talking to people – suppliers, customers, regulators, anyone that's in that food chain; listening to multiple points of view. Insight is incredibly important, but real insight usually requires experience.

'Insight is incredibly important, but real insight usually requires experience.'

BK: So what have been your biggest mistakes in business, investing, or life? And what did you learn from them?

JBL: Making mistakes is an incredible part of the learning process. We're constantly making mistakes as investment professionals because we're dealing with the unknown, the future – anything could happen tomorrow. All the time, we're making educated guesses. Considering the risks allows us to manage and minimise it.

'Making mistakes is an incredible part of the learning process.'

Very early on, when I was still at Foster Stockbroking, I remember I initiated coverage on Strathfield Car Radios. At the time, the retail environment was pretty good: consumers were feeling wealthy, so they were spending. In that kind of environment, all retailers tend to do well.

I remember thinking they looked a whole lot cheaper than the JB Hi-Fis out there and thought, 'Why wouldn't I buy this stock? It's trading pretty well, current commercial store growth is pretty good. Why wouldn't I go with a Buy recommendation?'

So I wrote the report, but didn't visit their stores; didn't experience the actual product. I remember Richard Uechtritz was running JB Hi-Fi back then, he'd just listed himself, and he came and saw me and said, 'Have you been to their store? Have you actually seen what the store looks like?'

*'When investments
perform poorly,
ultimately you have
no choice but to
pick yourself up
and work through it.'*

I went to the store and it didn't look great. I thought, 'Just trade it through', but all you need is a tougher consumer environment and everyone tightens their wallets. Think about JB Hi-Fi. It can continue to trade well even in a tougher environment because it's has a great format and management who understand what consumers want. That's what's so interesting about retailers. You can go to the store and experience the products; you can see if you like it and talk to people who actually buy them.

So that was one mistake I made; not doing the groundwork. I learned you have to see the product, touch it, feel it, and really know the story. As an investor, you need to know the business as if you're running it.

'As an investor, you need to know the business as if you're running it.'

BK: So what is Tribeca's strategy, and what role do you play?

JBL: We chose the name Tribeca because it is a place that's on the fringe of mainstream in New York. It's not downtown. It's innovative. It's different. That's how we see ourselves as well. At Tribeca, we constantly want to grow. We're growing across different asset classes using our expertise.

What's incredibly important for me with Tribeca is that when I run a fund, I feel ownership of it; it's my fund. I'm responsible for the performance. It's my reputation on the line if the fund doesn't work.

BK: If you could change one thing about your career, what would it be?

JBL: Every now and then I'll say I want to be a florist, but really, I don't want to change anything about my career. I enjoy it and I'm having fun.

Of course, there are times when it's quite a challenge, but when investments perform poorly, ultimately you have no choice but to pick yourself up and work through it. Once you've done that, it's an incredible feeling, isn't it? That's what life is all about. It's about going through challenges. Choose your path and push through; that's where you'll find your happiness.

'Choose your path and push through; that's where you'll find your happiness.'

BK: How do you balance having kids and a big career in this industry?

JBL: I do believe in quality time – on the weekends I spend as much time as possible with my two children; they're still very little. Then at work I try and be as focused as possible. I make it work.

It does mean that sometimes I work after my children have gone to bed because the time zone actually fits better, but for me, work is not something I just do in the office, it's part of me. My family is also part of me. It's just something that you find the best way to fit in.

'Work is not something I just do in the office, it's part of me. My family is also part of me. It's just something that you find the best way to fit in.'

BK: Do you think that technology has made working easier? You've got an office at home; you've got an office in your pocket.

JBL: Yes, absolutely. Without the advances in technology, working would be much more difficult – time in the office has become less important which is perfect given the other demands on my time.

Technology makes it possible for me to access prices or my portfolio anywhere. I have Bloomberg everywhere; I can set up, put out orders; call my dealer to do just about everything. I can do it anywhere; it makes working with international markets and different time zones much easier. It's life, for me, and it works.

BK: So why do you think there are less women in senior investment roles? Do you see that changing?

JBL: Yes, I see it changing. A lot of businesses are becoming increasingly flexible. It's not so much about part time and full time – we all know this job is not a part-time role; the markets don't sleep, so you've got to be constantly on.

The mentality that needs to change for women is the flexibility around where you work. If you can work from home after your children have gone to bed, or on the weekend, that will make it work a lot better. For me, it's an evolving process.

Perceptions, especially women's, will change, and businesses will provide more flexibility. Perception is very important. It used to be that how much time you spent at work equated to how hard you were working. That's changing! These days I find it's more about good performance. If you can deliver, if you can perform and get the work done. Where I do the work is not important.

'The mentality that needs to change for women is the flexibility around where you work.'

BK: That's an interesting point because ultimately, investment management is about performance – you can test that theory of what work is. Is it being in an office? Is it being in a coffee shop? Is it potentially watching your kids play sport or do the swimming carnival? A lot of people seem to have quite fixed views about what work is.

JBL: That's a very good point. For me, funds management, even being an analyst, is about understanding companies – rarely do I actually sit at my desk unless I have to finish reports, but even those I might do somewhere else.

I'm constantly talking to people; my diary is always full. I'll be talking to an industry contact, or management I met recently, and extracting information. Information is incredibly important. From information investors draw insights, information is instrumental to modelling financial forecasts and determining our fundamental view on a company. That insight is gained by talking to people – not from sitting at a desk. It's gained from visiting stores and being at industry conferences and meeting people.

BK: By visiting the store.

JBL: That's right! Anyone can sit in the office and look at financial statements. But doing your groundwork is what can really make a difference. If you really love certain segments, it makes it that little bit easier to get insight.

BK: In terms of lessons for investing, are there some key rules that you've gained? You've talked about visiting the site, touching the product, meeting the people, but what are the things that aren't necessarily in a spreadsheet that come to mind when you look at a company?

JBL: Management is incredibly important. You need to do a lot of research into management; understand how they think and look at their track record. The success of a business comes down to people and systems – the systems are really there to assist the people.

Having the right CEO and executive team really sets the tone for the culture of the business; that's extremely important. A lot of investors follow a strong management if they move to another company; but you still have to do your work because sometimes part of the success of management could be luck, but generally, management is what makes it happen. That is the number one rule.

If I feel suspicious or uncomfortable with how management operates, I will be very cautious. Even if the company is amazing, and seemingly has everything going for it; if the culture is poor in time things are more likely to go wrong and often enough they tend to fail. The importance of corporate culture is fascinating.

I recently listened to Dan Ariely, he's a famous American from Duke University. He recommends that businesses don't pay people bonuses because it doesn't work. He set up a fund just based on a list of measures of how well businesses are treating their people. He set up a score for all the companies in the S&P 500.

Then he literally set up a fund to buy companies in the top tier, and short the companies in the bottom tier. It was based purely on how businesses treat their employees. Whether they're paid fairly and is pay transparent, how are employees rewarded. Such measures are not captured in the financial measures investors typically observe. The portfolio took no account of the typical financial measures and ratios, it didn't even consider debt levels, none of the usual red flags.

His portfolio's performance – at least the model – was phenomenal. It goes to show that management is very important – especially how they treat their employees. So that's the first step: trust the management. Then you move on and do your homework. Once you've done that, don't worry about what other people are saying. The market is noisy, it's full of noise.

Take a longer-term view. If brokers are talking about some issue, or if you're seeing it in the paper, it means everyone already knows. It's in the price. If it's a negative story, this can be a good time to buy. Take a longer-term view; don't be afraid. You will make your return as long as you have done your homework.

'Take a longer-term view; don't be afraid. You will make your return as long as you have done your homework.'

BK: What do you call a good return, a great return, an excellent return?

JBL: Five percent is a bit small for me! Warren Buffet looks for a low-growth business, say 5 per cent and then he gears it up, which works because it's low volatility, it gives you that magnified return. But I like a company that is offering at least 10-15 per cent upside. That's the kind of company I like, but it depends.

Sometimes a company can be very, very cheap. It may be growing at 5 per cent, may be growing at 2 per cent, but it has very defensive earnings and it's trading at a steep discount and the market's missing the value. Then it's worthwhile.

Maybe the market isn't really forecasting the right return. When the market does start focusing on it, that's when you generate your returns. So for me, I'm

DEFINING CAREER MOMENT
- Jun Bei Liu -

When I was first appointed lead portfolio manager of the Alpha Plus fund, I travelled around Australia to see my clients and promised them I would look after their clients' lifesavings. With every handshake, I was determined to deliver for those clients, not only for their faith in me but the enormous fiduciary duty they and their clients have entrusted in me. That was a career defining moment. We need to remind ourselves that we operate in such an important industry, and that our investment performance will directly impact the retirement savings of many Australians. We should thrive to do better every day.

looking for 10-15 per cent. Whether it's from the market mispricing a stock, or it's from the company growing at that rate plus a little bit of dividend. I'm looking for a good return profile.

Of course, often we look for shorter term catalysts. Sometimes you can find a company which is too expensive, which can offer a good opportunity to short the name.

BK: Where do you think your return comes from in your fund at the moment, long versus short?

JBL: We generate reasonably balanced returns from both long and short positions over a longer investment period. The contribution varies with market conditions, especially in the short term, for example during a period of sharp selloff, we can see material return from the short book and vice versa.

BK: Is it really a hedge fund?

JBL: It is not fully hedged. We offer active hedge fund return in addition to the market returns. We target at least 5 per cent outperformance vs the ASX200.

BK: So you are 50/50?

JBL: We own 150 per cent worth of shares by shorting 50 per cent shares. So we can benefit from both rising and falling share prices.

BK: Are you active with short in the sense that you're not taking a public position on your short?

JBL: Sometimes we can be vocal about our positions simply as we look to educate other investors of the opportunities or pitfalls. As an investor, we sometimes can take an activist approach when we feel our advice can add value to increase shareholder returns. But we don't do that publicly, we generally work closely with the management.

In terms of the short positions, we are reasonably open about some of our higher conviction names. We short companies for various reasons, from earnings quality to stretched valuations and sometimes to balance our exposure or reduce risks in a particular sector.

BK: How are you trying to play technology from an investment point of view?

JBL: We like the technology sector, it offers enormous growth opportunities relative to other sectors, particularly as many of these businesses are capital light and offer high returns on equity. The sector is very expensive driven by scarcity as

investors hunt for growth. We believe the best way to participate in the growth is via a long short strategy. Buy the companies that offer a solid and clear path to growth and short the ones that could be challenged by future disruptions.

Unlike many long only managers that are struggling with valuation support in this sector, we are comfortable to take advantage of this period of strong price performance, boosting our returns, while managing the volatility with short positions.

BK: Because the prices are off a lot. I think Apple's down 30 per cent.

JBL: Yes, but its earnings have come off as well, so you have to be careful about that. Expensive stocks tend to be very volatile around changes in earnings growth expectations, so it is crucial to get the earnings forecasts right. We are now seeing increasing polarisation within the sector as investors are paying more for those that deliver vs those which disappoint, a long short strategy can works particularly well in this environment.

BK: So it's more a mismatch between expectations that are not necessarily built or promoted by the companies, it's more the herd gets excited.

JBL: That's right, exactly. You need to work out what the market is expecting and what the company can realistically deliver – it's two pieces. Investors need to do the homework and assess the expectation differential before making investment decisions.

'Investors need to do the homework and assess the expectation differential before making investment decisions.'

BK: And then, what about Asia? You have ambition for expanding investment horizon to Asia. What makes that unique and interesting?

JBL: For me, first of all, I love the consumer sector; it's a sector that is so visible. And it's somewhere I've had a lot of investment experience in as well as strong industry contacts. Asia offers the largest and fastest growing consumer and technology market, we simply can not ignore its vast opportunity set as well as its enormous importance to the future of the global economy.

I have ambition to expand our investment scope in the next few years to include Asia and offer our investors opportunities to participate in the enormous growth.

BK: Every Asian country's middle class, in fact.

JBL: Exactly. In 10 years' time, the spend will reach $11 trillion just from China, from the Chinese middle class. India is somewhere similar, an incredible growth. By then 60% of the total global consumer spend will come out of emerging Asia. That is where the growth will be and that's where you want to allocate your capital. The consumer spend from OECD countries such Australia, the US, Europe and Japan will account for a small portion of the global pie. All that investment is going to go to the Asian consumer – that's where the dollar is going; that's opportunity.

'All that investment is going to go to the Asian consumer –

that's where the dollar is going; that's opportunity.

BK: When you speak of that market, does that mean globally you will invest in any company that has exposure to that growth?

JBL: Absolutely.

BK: So your LVMHs, your EMEAs, these sorts of people?

JBL: Partly, but rather than just retailers, I want to include technology and other exciting sectors as well. As you can see, in the emerging Asian market, there are a lot of new categories and companies that fall into the broader consumer sector, which is quite unique for the Asian markets.

BK: There's quite a lot of talk that more than 50 per cent of the top 500 US companies' earnings are global. Will you end up with a group of companies that look very similar to what already exists? Will they be Asian companies, will they be US companies, European companies, or just any company that has that exposure?

JBL: Our aim is at some point when we are ready to expand our investment universe, we will offer our investors majority Australian portfolio enhanced with Asian opportunities. This will be a much lower risk and potential higher return strategy for investors to participate in the Asian consumer growth.

The opportunities are vast, with so many new business models in Asia. Look at Amazon, despite being an innovator of the online retailing sector, they are now learning from how Alibaba and JD are charging customers for the media spend in Asia, they're actually looking at their business models.

BK: Do you think that if you're investing in Australian companies that have been around a long time, in a public market context, their governance and culture is different to early-stage Asian companies.

JBL: Absolutely.

BK: The Japanese have a long history of running these large, publicly listed companies, but when I look at China, it does make me nervous.

JBL: Absolutely. We need to remember that China is an emerging economy. Economic structure is still being refined and its government is doing its best to steer the country towards long-term stability and growth. We probably would have asked the same questions of the Japanese companies a few decades ago when their economy was rising through the ranks. With that in mind, it's critical to manage risks when investing in Asia, particularly emerging Asia. A long short strategy with majority Australian companies is a safe way to gain exposure to the enormous opportunities we spoke about.

'We need to remember that China is an emerging economy. Economic structure is still being refined and its government is doing its best to steer the country towards long-term stability and growth.'

BK: And certainly when we see people trying to make money in China, that looks interesting. India's the same.

JBL: Yes, absolutely, I think that's very important. For me, being Australian but coming from China, I can see a lot of cultural differences. That's why when you look from the outside, all these government reforms look quite scary. But you need to see what they're trying to do from the inside; you need to know how the culture works. If you talk to experts that actually live in China and ask questions about the uncertainty in terms of regulatory changes, they talk to a stable framework. The government has a broad plan and tends to provide quite clear guidance as to it long term goals. One example I can give you is the "beautiful China" initiative. The government outlined the initiative for several years before actual implementing changes such as restrictions on pollution. Most foreign investors dismissed the initial statement as immaterial and didn't believe the government would follow through on such a disruptive project.

BK: Because they're used to Western politicians.

JBL: That's right. Our politicians say things but don't follow through or plans change as their popularity waxes and wanes, whereas in China they can take a very long-term view. When they outline the policy to clean up the environment, trust they will get it done. They are investing in clean energy projects, encouraging capital flow into environment friendly companies and shutting down pollution plants, all just in a mere few years.

Therefore the key is to be on the ground, understand how it works, have the right contacts into those markets, and really be on top of what's happening. Take Chinese share market as an example, it has been very volatile due to the 70 per cent retail participation, but the share market in China is actually a very good indication of consumer confidence.

'The key is to be on the ground, understand how it works, have the right contacts into those markets, and really be on top of what's happening.'

So when the market rallies strongly, we should expect stronger retail spend to come through. Understanding those links is important and can prove valuable. You really need to know what's happening on the ground, rather than just looking in from the outside.

BK: Jun Bei, thank you so much.

INVESTMENT WISDOM LESSONS

• Separate sentiment from reality

Share prices movements occur in the short term by the sentiment or mood of the investors. Market downturns should be used as buying opportunities, because long term returns will ultimately be driven by the underlying fundamentals.

• Beware of "hot tips"

"Hot tips" are dangerous. It generally means many investors have caught onto the idea, and that investor then risk overpaying for the stock at this late stage.

• Don't be afraid to be contrarian

Investments that will generate the biggest return are often contrarian ideas, although thorough due diligence of the investment is critical when going against the herd.

Paul Moore

Chairman and Chief Investment Officer, PM Capital

'I've always been pretty frugal. Mum says I probably still have my first 20 cents of pocket money – but from that saving mentality, you become an investor.'

Paul Moore is known to invest with patience and conviction, ignoring short-term market trends to uncover mispriced assets in industries as diverse as brewing, banking and casinos, in countries from the US to Ireland and Argentina.

He began his career in 1985 as an industrial equity analyst. In 1986 he became Portfolio Manager of the BT Select Markets American Growth Fund - acknowledged as one of the sector's leading mutual funds.

From 1994 to 1998, Paul assumed responsibility for the BT Split Trust and BT Select Markets International Trust – two of Australia's best performing global equities funds. During this time, he was also head of BT's Retail International Equity Group, which was awarded International Equity Manager of the Year in 1995 and 1996.

Paul established PM Capital in 1998 and developed the investment philosophy and process that has underpinned the company's excess return generation since its inception.

Paul holds a Bachelor of Commerce (Honours) degree, majoring in Finance from the University of New South Wales.

www.pmcapital.com.au

Interview

BRETT KELLY: Paul, you often talk about investing ahead of inflection points. What is an inflection point?

PAUL MOORE: Assessing the current status of an investment alone isn't going to make you money. You need to be able to see something that other people don't see, or anticipate change – positive or negative – that others don't see coming.

Whether it's the Aussie dollar or a stock, generally there are ten-year cycles in investment markets. When a really good business goes through tough macro- or industry-specific issues, you will typically get a downturn in terms of revenue and earnings. When this occurs, people start to think that the status quo is permanent – particularly if it's an extended downturn – when in fact it's transitory.

When these factors come into play they cause a trough in the industry. In other words, an inflection point. However, right at the bottom of any inflection point, when the news can be at its darkest, that close watchers can actually see signs of life. It's the classic light at the end of the tunnel.

Moreover, if you can buy when that maximum valuation discount coincides with the trough (at the inflection point), that's when you make real money – provided you've got a proper time horizon.

'When these factors come into play they cause a trough in the industry. In other words, an inflection point.'

BK: What's a proper time horizon?

PM: It's different for everyone, but I've found that there's a two- or three-year period when the market doesn't want to believe that trends are inflecting. That's the hardest part because the stock can keep going down even though the fundamentals are improving (they can go sideways too).

If you're right on that inflection, however, you'll start getting positive news. A little bit, then a bit more. It's in that three- to five-year period that the market really starts to focus on it and then, when you get to years six and seven, the market's accepting of the good news. They start to re-rate it, and can actually get comfortable with it. Then, somewhere in the seven- to ten-year period, they overvalue it, which is time to sell.

My observations are that somewhere in that five- to ten-year mark is the sweet spot to sell. That's why we say that seven years is the minimum you need to take advantage of these genuine long-term opportunities. I've found that they typically take about ten years, plus or minus.

My first big investment was Wells Fargo. It was a classic – a great business – but back then, it wasn't very well known.

BK: That was in the late '80s, before Bob Joss came to run Westpac.

PM: Correct. I first came across Bob Joss when he was at Wells Fargo.

BK: That's when I bought my first stock: Westpac.

PM: Yes, my first big investment experience was very early in my career. I went over to the US to look at all the banking stocks. It was right at the tail-end of the savings and loan crisis when all the commercial banks were in trouble.

I remember being in a bank in Boston and the staff there were stressed because the regulators were in there. I didn't realise it at the time, but they were deciding whether or not they would close the bank down. It was a pure fluke that we were there at the peak of the crisis. I was very young and naive in terms of my investment experience – it was a great learning opportunity. We stumbled across Wells Fargo – nobody knew who they were back then.

The thing that stood out was the unbelievable deposit franchise. Basically, the east coast of the US was where the population grew first. There were lots of banks – lots of competition for deposits – so you tended to get a 1 per cent to 1.5 per cent deposit margin. But when you went to California, which was developed after World War II, you only had a few banks; Wells Fargo had a 4 per cent-plus deposit margin. They had this wonderful deposit margin that protected their downside, plus they were great credit underwriters.

People were worried about them precisely because they were commercial property underwriters. At that time California was at the peak of the commercial property crisis. It was on the front page of Barron's as the "great short of the century".

BK: As a diversion, Vernon Hill says what makes banks great is that they are a regulated opportunity to get deposits cheaply; they are a deposit franchise.

PM: Correct. Wells Fargo not only had a deposit franchise, but the number one deposit franchise in America. It not only survived, but went on to thrive and become acknowledged as one of the very best banks in the industry. That's why in times of financial crisis, we look for banks with strong domestic deposit franchises. Having said that, looking at ten years plus, it is probably the first time these deposit franchises may be under threat. We may be at an inflection point.

'Looking at ten years plus, it is probably the first time these deposit franchises may be under threat. We may be at an inflection point.'

BK: Interestingly, in light of the Royal Commission, there's not much more you could have done to blow yourself up, but they're still there. Those brands are potentially under-appreciated in terms of their strength.

PM: We're in an industry where, as a general rule, we're overpaid relative to other industries. And if you have a lack of leadership you can have a lack of people who are willing to do the right thing – it's human nature. That's why we ended up with the Royal Commission. Leaders are supposed to understand human nature and lead by example.

BK: So how do you invest?

PM: The basics haven't really changed from the day I started; I rely on instinct and valuation. I've always thought if I can get a 10 per cent a year return, I'll do okay through the power of compounding. You want to beat cash and the index because otherwise you may as well put your money in the bank or in an index fund and then go to the beach every day. Then it's about finding businesses that have been mispriced by the market. I never instinctively go out to actually outperform the MSCI. What I do is find companies that appear to be mispriced.

BK: So you're looking for a 10 per cent discounted margin of safety?

PM: A 10 per cent return.

BK: Are you trying to do that when buying?

PM: Yes, bottom line. If you've got a business that's giving a 10 per cent return year in, year out, hallelujah.

'If you've got a business that's giving a 10 per cent return year in, year out, hallelujah.'

BK: Through dividends and capital growth?

PM: Yes. The way we look at it is to take the view that we are buying the whole business. As an owner, am I getting a 10 per cent return per year on my capital. Now, the returns may be even – 10 per cent / 10 per cent / 10 per cent. We'd love that kind of return profile, but typically, it's two steps forward, one step back – 20 per cent / 20 per cent / -10 per cent, for example. Or it can be 0 per cent / 0 per cent / 30 per cent.

Generally, we're looking at a three- to five-year period – that's where things are mispriced. You're actually looking for something that might be mispriced by 40 to 50 per cent. In other words, in five years' time, if it was back to normal conditions and normal valuation, it could be 50 per cent higher. That's 10 per cent a year.

It's roughly that sort of framework. The Wells Fargo experience taught me that you find the best opportunities in the biggest crisis. The only problem is, you've got to have the ability to back your convictions.

BK: See beyond the crisis!

PM: Yes, and also deal with everyone telling you that you're wrong in the short term. Often the stock goes against you in the short term, so you really have to have that discipline. We arbitrage people's lack of patience. Everyone can look at a business; there's plenty of smart people to do all the quantitative analysis.

BK: It's the return for character.

PM: Again, I learnt that with Wells Fargo. Being young and naive, I was buying these financial companies in my US equity fund – back then, I had 60-70 per cent in financials – and that was before we had all these external gatekeepers putting all those constraints on you. In the first month of the fund it was really close to the bottom, but it was just coincidence. We built up these positions in financial stocks, but very near to the first month, financials kept going down and the market was actually recovering. The fund was down 5 per cent and the market might have been up around 7 per cent.

BK: And the boss put the piece of paper on your desk to explain yourself?

PM: Yes. At the time, I was in my early to mid-twenties. They were very fixated in the short-term numbers so the pressure was on. To be a good investor, you have to have a bit of stubbornness, and be able to back your conviction. Over the next five years, it was the best performing mutual fund in the country because of those financial stocks. That just highlights how you have to have the ability to do the work properly. If you don't, you get weak at the knees when people start putting ideas into your head.

'Some of my worst mistakes have been due to external influences; when I haven't done the work properly or didn't trust my conviction'

*'To be a good investor, you have to have a bit of stubbornness.
You have to have the ability to do the work properly.
If you don't, you get weak at the knees when people
start putting ideas into your head.'*

Some of my worst mistakes have been due to external influences; when I haven't done the work properly or didn't trust my conviction. You've got to have a strong backbone. The best ideas I've ever seen and invested in were severely questioned, even ridiculed. If you're the sort of person that needs to get love from the crowd, you're not going to be a good investor. Consensus investing is a recipe for disaster because, by definition, the risk / reward's gone.

You've got to be doing something different from the rest of the crowd. The reality is, if they question you, you're probably on the right track. But you have to do the work: just picking non-consensus ideas or contrarian ideas doesn't work. When you do the work, you can realise there's a reason why a stock is trading like it is. If you look at what you do differently, there's a reward for patience; there's a reward for character in terms of being prepared to find that difference and back it.

*'If you're the sort of person that needs to get love from the crowd,
you're not going to be a good investor.'*

BK: Can you redeem daily with the unlisted PM Capital Global Companies Fund, and with the listed investment company (LIC) PM Capital Global Opportunities Fund (ASX: PGF)?

PM: Yes, daily. A difference being that the LIC is a closed-end fund, permanent capital, so we don't have to be concerned with day to day cash flows, giving us more control over the investment decision.

BK: With the LIC structure, how much was raised?

PM: Around $300 million, plus or minus.

BK: How do you educate your investors to stick with you in a down period?

PM: It's a constant process. Our clients are really the advisors, who then have

their clients, so you're not in direct contact with the ultimate investor. That's the hardest part. It's very simple: you look at flows in to and out of mutual funds, no matter what category.

I guarantee what you'll find is that you get the most people flying in at the top and the most people flying out at the bottom. It's hard to stop the crowd when it's running the other way.

'It's hard to stop the crowd when it's running the other way.'

BK: Will you continue to run both LICs and funds long term?

PM: The permanent capital provided by LICs means we're in total control of the investment decision. Initially, we had he unlisted trust because that's our core. Then we found that investors were moving to self-managed super funds and going direct. That's why we brought out the LIC. It's the same strategy, it just depends on the client and what they prefer.

BK: How much money is in the unlisted total?

PM: Around $450 million [to end April, 2019].

BK: So why wouldn't you just change the business?

PM: We've got clients that have been with us for a long time who prefer the unlisted space, then we've got clients who prefer the listed; it's their choice. In the unlisted space, you have to have daily redemptions as a requirement to be placed on certain platforms. In a perfect world, from a pure investment perspective you'd just have a captive vehicle so there is more control over the investment decision.

'In a perfect world, you'd just have a captive vehicle so there is more control over the investment decision.'

BK: What stops you from doing that?

PM: There's a client base that prefers to use the unlisted trust. They have the ability to take it out if they want to. In the LIC, you've got the captive money, but then the problem is they can sell at a discount.

BK: But you can buy it back.

PM: We can. But ideally you don't want your shareholders selling at a discount. In terms of keeping the client educated in times of stress so that they don't make irrational decisions, you've got the same problem in both vehicles. Ultimately, your client will make the decision; it's beyond your control.

BK: Yes, a key battle. What did you study at university?

PM: I studied commerce but really, to be a good investor, you need to be born with that saving DNA. I've always been pretty frugal. Mum says I probably still have my first 20 cents of pocket money – but from that saving mentality, you become an investor.

'I've always been pretty frugal. Mum says I probably still have my first 20 cents of pocket money – but from that saving mentality, you become an investor.'

When I was in high school, I bought a few shares in Blue Metal Industries, which was taken over by Boral. It was peanuts, but I had a good experience. Then when I was at university, I invested that money in Carlton & United Breweries, which was bought out by Elders IXL. It's either in your DNA or it's not.

BK: So after your degree, you went to BT?

PM: Yes, I got a job in their investment division in 1985.

BK: Was Kerr Neilson there at the time?

PM: Yes, he was my first boss.

BK: What did you learn in that team that's been influential over your career?

PM: It played to my natural instinct – I was encouraged to think in the longer term; to look for how things should be rather than the way they were.

'I was encouraged to think in the longer term; to look for how things should be rather than the way they were.'

Early on I felt like a fish out of water because they were very short-term in nature; very relative. It was a top-down macro approach and I'm more of a natural stock picker, but it happened to coincide with when they set up their select equity markets trusts. Kerr is a stock picker by nature too so he was given the opportunity to do that and asked me to help him. I was given the American growth fund and he did the rest. It was a great learning curve for me because I was thrown in the deep end. The US equity market is the broadest market in the world; it's the best place to work. And Kerr was much longer-term, much more stock-specific, versus the macro approach, so I could observe the two different styles.

BK: So more of a trading style.

PM: Yes. Macro top-down trading. That's where I learned the pros and cons of long-term investing, which really suited my skill set. There was a lot of pressure, but I learned that's when you're most vulnerable to making a mistake longer term.

BK: How long did you work for Kerr in that environment?

PM: He left in 1993 or 1994 and then I took over responsibility. I was there for another three years before setting up PM Capital in 1998. Right from the start I saw myself doing my own thing. That was reinforced by working in a big institution because the bigger an organisation becomes, the more political it becomes, and they stray from the real essence of it. I just wanted to invest. I'm not a political person. I tend to say what I think, particularly when I was young and hadn't learned the ropes. I'm not the kind of person that works well in a big institution. I was always destined to do my own thing.

'I'm not the kind of person that works well in a big institution. I was always destined to do my own thing.'

BK: How old were you when you started PM Capital?

PM: I was 32, which was quite young. I didn't realise it at the time.

BK: So what was the vision for the business?

PM: It was a very simple proposition – still is. We think we can add value to your portfolio. We try to explain to people what we do and why we do it. If there's an alignment, please consider us as an investment manager. We do things differently. We have a different time horizon. We invest in different things to most.

It's not just the long-term return, but different risk characteristics. Typically, we're performing when others may not be and vice versa. It's about diversity. If you can bring different characteristics, that's true diversification.

'Typically, we're performing when others may not be and vice versa. It's about diversity. If you can bring different characteristics, that's true diversification.'

BK: How is the business compared to what you'd hoped it would be?

PM: The ultimate aim is to invest your own capital, and if you do that well, the reality is that your clients are going to have the same experience and you have a good business. We're a little bit different from most people out there. We don't prioritise the business side where managers just want to grow their funds under management (FUM). I'd rather focus on the investment side. I'm the largest investor in our funds.

BK: It follows that, over time, if you deliver the returns, to a degree you'll get the FUM.

PM: In theory you should, but it's been a pretty powerful oligopoly out there with the banks, insurance companies and so on. We've had plenty of advisors that want to use us, and the banks and the insurance companies just say no because they've got their own product. Obviously, they'll get more fees if they put it in their own product. That's the reason we had a Royal Commission. But, yes, there's a business side to it. We need to communicate and talk to the advisors – that's why we've got a CEO and a sales force – but ultimately, what I've always wanted to do was invest.

BK: What's the future?

PM: Obviously, you accumulate your own capital, so I suspect I'll be investing until the day I die. Eventually, I'll do less on the business side and more just investing the capital, but I'm only approaching the halfway mark. We have individuals who are coming up through the ranks, so I expect they will start taking responsibility for some of the funds. But they have to earn the right to run the global fund.

From a business perspective, you don't want to be in a position where as the CIO you get hit by a bus and everything falls over. You want clients to continue to be able to receive the same experience in terms of the philosophy and process.

BK: What is the future of index and active management?

PM: It's an interesting one. For the average investor, index funds may be an easy way to do it. But we can do better. The Global Companies Fund's return since inception is 464 per cent versus the index's 170 per cent [to end April, 2019], so we've been able to add real value over the longer term. My natural instincts are always to do better than the average. Passive dominates now, but it is no longer an easy solution. It's become so big, and whenever that happens, it's no longer going to give you an acceptable rate of return. What that means is if passive returns are going to be sub-normal, you need active managers. We think in the next few years you are going to get average returns of between 0 per cent and 2 per cent on cash, 0 per cent to 3 per cent on bonds, and 3 per cent to 5 per cent on equities. You could do your typical blended asset allocation, but you're going to get 2 to 3 per cent returns at best. Take away the fees and you're not going to make any money. You need active now.

BK: That's pre-inflation returns.

PM: Yes, and it's going to be tough to earn a return right at the point when everyone's piling into bonds and passive equities. You need to find good, active investors. People underestimate just how pervasive it is because you not only have passive exchange traded funds, but the vast majority of institutional active managers have weightings that are very close to the index. That's why the next three years are going to be really interesting because you've had this huge 30-year trend in interest rates turning around and a huge swerve to passive. When interest rates go back up, you have less liquidity, which is going to create a wider dispersion in long-term opportunities. That's great for active guys, provided you've got the right time horizon. I would now argue that passive's no longer going to do the job for the average investor.

BK: What people dressed up as money management, actually isn't.

PM: The industry's shot itself in the foot; they didn't have the character to say no.

BK: It was pretty easy for a long time. It was hard to be an index fund investor 10 years ago, but it isn't now and it will get easier. So the herd in the middle...

PM: It's gone. You've got to be genuinely active or you may as well be passive.

BK: I've noticed across industries that essentially, the middle is dead.

PM: You've got to communicate what you believe in and follow up with actions that are consistent with your beliefs.

'You've got to communicate what you believe in and follow up with actions that are consistent with your beliefs.'

BK: It's the biggest issue – aligning beliefs, words and actions.

PM: What the regulators and the government and the industry leaders don't understand is that if you let a little thing slip, that's what creates bad culture, which leads to bad actions. If you deal with something little upfront, it never gets the opportunity to grow.

BK: What have you've learned from your greatest failures?

PM: Firstly, that I need to back my instinct, and secondly, to do the work – the final 1 per cent makes all the difference.

Probably the biggest mistake you can make as an investor is when a thesis isn't turning out the way you expected. The first reaction to something going wrong is to sell. You have to fight against that instinct. You need to be calm and measured, and revisit your original investment case.

There's a constant battle between what's going to happen tomorrow and being methodical about what has happened in the past and why. The reality is you've got to keep guarding against all these things – it's not as if you make the mistake and then you never make it again.

It's also very easy to get caught up in being busy. You keep falling into that trap because it's a 24/7 job. To try any counteract that, once we've done all the work we write an investment summary so that when there's a red flag we can go back and reassess – not react.

That's what will keep you invested when you get distracting market noise.

On the flipside, hopefully that's what will get you out when things start going wrong. You go back to your thesis and you reassess given the new information. The biggest mistake you can make is thinking you can hold out for a better price when a stock has fallen. If the thesis is broken, then it's time to get out.

'The biggest mistake you can make is thinking you can hold out for a better price when a stock has fallen. If the thesis is broken, then it's time to get out.'

'I've got the benefit of being around for the last 30 years. I can work out who's been lucky and who hasn't.'

BK: Other investors write their thesis, then they make their investments. And then they change their thesis to suit what they've done!

PM: Ultimately, I've got to be responsible, which is why we also keep a record of ideas and recommendations. If you go back to our quarterly report, you can go back ten years and look at when we first talked about a certain company and why we bought it. I'm not going to lie, we all like to save face – it's human nature – but if you want to be a good investor, you need to learn how to deal with that and the best way to do so is to commonly revisit why you bought it in the first place.

'If you go back to our quarterly report, you can go back ten years and look at when we first talked about a certain company and why we bought it.'

BK: We put together a case study on a big hedge fund that records every conversation and films every meeting; they have a bunch of data people working on it full time. When they have an idea and execute it, and then make money, they want to be able to go back and ascertain whether they were lucky or brilliant.

PM: That's the thing. You can look back and know you got something 100 per cent right in terms of what you were trying to achieve. And you can look at the ones you got wrong and work out the mistakes you made and what you need to avoid in future. If you've written it down, you can remind yourself. It's the best learning tool.

I still reflect on the ones where I was right and the ones I got wrong. Sometimes it takes a little while to deal with the ones you got wrong because you don't like to remind yourself of what an idiot you were and how you didn't stick to your disciplines.

'I still reflect on the ones I got right as well as the ones I got wrong.'

BK: You learn more from your mistakes.

PM: It really is a long-term game. You'll have your ups and downs. There are days when people will think you're a superstar, and days they'll think you're a mug. The bottom line is, you have to have good a fundamental framework.

'The bottom line is, you have to have a good fundamental framework.'

The dropout rate for the industry is very high. People tend to look at who's had really good returns this year, or in the last five years. But how many people are still in the business after 20 years? Not many.

People often make the mistake of equating good performance with being a good fund manager. I've got the benefit of being around for the last 30 years. I can work out who's been lucky and who hasn't. Sometimes people go through a rough patch, but they're excellent investors of capital – you've got to be careful not to jump to the wrong conclusions too early.

There's nothing like the benefit of hindsight. It should reinforce what you need to do to be a good investor of capital and reinforce the mistakes you've got to avoid. Otherwise it's like playing roulette – you don't know why you won, you don't know why you lost; you just keep hoping you'll get the next one right.

BK: Often, people might be hugely successful, but when they go to the next thing, they just do the same thing when the circumstances or environment have totally changed.

PM: And they blow up. It's like some Australian fund managers going global. You're in the real world then. The US market is very different to the Australian market - there's no inside information and you've got the smartest people in the world. It's a tough business. Look at how many of them have gone offshore and it hasn't worked. I was fortunate to learn that really early on, just by accident. If you're going to go offshore, whether funds management or whatever, you have to understand the fundamentals of success there. It's almost like starting again.

BK: What are the things that you can clearly identify that you shouldn't do?

PM: One of the biggest dangers of being a fund manager, and we all go through it, is when you make a good investment and think you're pretty clever. You need to learn to focus on where you're good. You can't be good at all things; you've got to recognise where you've got an advantage over others and where you don't.

'You can't be good at all things: you've got to recognise where you've got an advantage over others and where you don't.'

If I can't break it down to something that's very simple, then I shouldn't be investing. But the bottom line is we're all victims to it. You do something well, you think you're pretty smart, and you get a big head. That's why a lot drop out. They get a bit of success, aren't aware of the risk, and eventually they blow up.

It's life, isn't it? You've got to be able to reflect on your experiences and bring it back to the centre in terms of a balanced view on what's happened and what you need to do and what you don't need to do. Investing is no different.

BK: If there was a motto, quote or thought that best summarises your approach to life in investing, what would it be?

PM: Investing is just simple ideas, simple businesses. Every time I stray from that, I get anything from a bloody nose to being kicked somewhere painful. The beauty is that when we find those simple ideas, we can play it in so many different ways, in different geographies. Nine times out of ten, you find an idea that's repeating itself all around the world, but maybe on time lapse. Over time, that's what I've driven: the backing of simple ideas, simple businesses, many iterations.

The real motto for me is to not doubt your conviction. The financial services industry is a classic. There's so much temptation to stray from the path that you know is right because there's too much money flying around.

'The real motto for me is, don't doubt your conviction.'

BK: Do you have a short-term vision?

PM: I avoid short termism in investing and in life. That's got all those people into trouble – trying to make money in the short term, instead of asking, is this right or wrong?

BK: A reputation takes 20 years to gain...

PM: A lot of these people in financial services know they're doing the wrong thing, but they either think they can get away with it, or everyone else is doing it. You've got to have character because in the end you've got to look yourself in the mirror. You've got to be able to say, 'I don't care if everyone else is doing it, I think this is wrong. I'm going to communicate it to everyone and I'm not going to do it.'

BK: Clients can't get that capital back; they can't get the time back.

PM: People work hard to save money. We have a custodial responsibility to do what's right, what's in their best interest. It's not about getting as much money out of them and into our pocket; we're there to look after them.

BK: Who's the right custodian for Australians' pensions? The free market? Government?

PM: I'm 100 per cent someone who takes responsibility for their own investing. To me, that's a great system. It also solves a long-term issue of government because it forces savings and people can better look after themselves.

What the government has to understand is that if you force someone to save, you have to ensure that money is managed in the best interest of those clients. It hasn't achieved that.

If you look at any industry, wherever you get a concentration of power, you get a bad outcome. So originally, where did all the money congregate? Insurance companies – but they all blew up in corruption and people went to jail.

All the money is now going into industry super funds and you're getting another concentration of power. I said to people five years ago that the next big blow up is going to be in industry super funds because they are gaining a concentration of power. You can already see it happening – they're all going into these alternative investments and private equity.

Industry funds have had a good run. The problem is that when interest rates inflate, which isn't a worry for the moment – it takes time for those pressures to build – but ten years down the track, I'm not sure it's a good idea for these guys to be buying direct assets like ports. That was the best-performing infrastructure for the last 30 years because of lower interest rates.

'Running a business is very different to investing in a business – I've learned that lesson as well.'

They think they're doing the right thing, but my gut tells me they're actually the crowd now and they're going in at the wrong time. After all, running a business is very different to investing in a business - I've learned that lesson as well.

In 10, 20 years, you're going to have some interesting observations and discussions about the superannuation industry because concentration of power always leads to trouble.

BK: Very good, thank you so much.

INVESTMENT WISDOM LESSONS

• Crisis can be good
You find the best opportunities in the biggest crisis.

• Remain convinced
You've got to have the ability to back your convictions.

• Advantage: you
You can't be good at all the things; you've got to recognise where you've got an advantage over others and where you don't.

John
Murray

Managing Director, Perennial Value

'Bringing people on the journey is really important.'

John Murray established Perennial Value in January 2000 and has some 30 years' industry experience. He is one of Australia's most respected value investors and has built a stable team of investment professionals who have delivered consistently strong results for investors.

Under John's leadership, funds under management have grown from $40 million in 2000 to current levels and Perennial Value has won a number of prestigious industry awards and accolades. In October 2014, John was inducted into the Australian Funds Management Hall of Fame.

https://perennial.net.au/our-story/

Interview

BRETT KELLY: I'd like to start at the beginning, John. Where did you grow up, what is your background?

JOHN MURRAY: Both my mother and father come from families of seven; they grew up in Canberra when it was much smaller. In fact, both my families farmed on some of the country that is now under Lake Burley Griffin. I grew up on a family sheep and cattle property about 30 miles south of Canberra, towards Cooma. I went to secondary school in Canberra, at St Edmund's College. My wife says that the only thing I learned to do at school was play rugby, I was captain of the First XV and Sportsman of the Year in my final year.

My education started around the kitchen table at our farm; my mother was my initial educator. Though we weren't far out of Canberra, half of the road was tarred and half of it was dirt road. In mid-winter, it became impassable at times, which meant we couldn't go to school on a daily basis; it was just too far away. So in the initial years – I am the eldest of four – we were taught by correspondence around the kitchen table. My mother taught me to be meticulous in terms of spelling, reading, writing and adding up, so I learnt the basics well! We spent the rest of our time helping on the farm and it was a simple and idyllic lifestyle for a child when I look back on my childhood.

'My education started around the kitchen table at our farm; my mother was my initial educator through correspondence school. She taught me to be meticulous in terms of spelling, reading, writing and adding up.'

BK: And then off to university?

JM: Yes, coming from families on both sides who were self-starters and had been through both good and very tough times as well, with droughts and variable beef and wool prices, I decided about halfway through high school that I didn't want to be a farmer. The only thing I knew that I wanted to do was be in business, but I didn't have any idea what that meant.

'I decided about halfway through high school that I didn't want to be a farmer. The only thing I knew that I wanted to do was be in business, but I didn't have any idea what that meant.'

So I did an accounting degree at what was then the Canberra College of Advanced Education. It's now called University of Canberra. I didn't know it when I left school, but the CCAE was one of a handful of top accounting courses in the country; it was pretty hard going because it was just something completely new to me.

BK: And then where did you start your working life?

JM: In Sydney at Price Waterhouse. I had to make a choice: I was offered a graduate accountant role at ICI, which is now Orica, at the head office at 1 Nicholson Street in Melbourne. The starting salary there was $15,000 – I'll never forget the letter of offer. I was also offered a job in Sydney at Price Waterhouse, in the Australian head office at 50 Bridge Street. The salary was $12,500. So I had a very big decision to make as the difference in salaries at the time was significant. I accepted the role at Price Waterhouse.

BK: Into audit, or tax?

JM: Yes, into audit. When it came to the final interview at Price Waterhouse, they flew me up from Canberra. I was interviewed by one of the senior partners on the 37th floor at 50 Bridge Street; it was a magnificent view of the harbour. I'd never been that high up in a building before. In fact, I'd rarely been to Sydney before – my whole life had been spent around Canberra. So that was at age 21. Of course, there were three or four of us being interviewed at the same time. I distinctly remember the other three – city born and bred – they answered the questions professionally while I spent most of the time looking out the window at the view. I was lucky enough to secure a job in audit. That was a very formative time. It was a lot of fun too, and I made some fantastic contacts, many of whom I still touch upon in life, and with my work now. That period as a chartered accountant with Price Waterhouse that it set me up for my future career.

'That period as a chartered accountant with Price Waterhouse set me up for my future career.'

BK: How many years did you spend there?

JM: A few of us moved on after about four years. We did the Professional Year, I also spent some time in insolvency and learnt a lot during that formative time.

BK: The only bloke to have found audit boring.

JM: Yes, that's right, we're quite rare!

BK: And then where did you go?

JM: In the mid-'80s, I joined Bankers Trust as a credit analyst. At that time, Keating and Hawke were in power deregulating the Australian economy, there were all sorts of opportunities for investment banks. It was a pretty heady period; another formative period.

BK: Were the staff at Bankers Trust ex-Price Waterhouse?

JM: There were chartered accountants there, that's true, however these were professionals from many and diverse backgrounds. At Bankers Trust, the credit department I worked in was independent from the rest of the business. It was one of the few banks in Australia – both trading banks and investment banks – that actually had an independent credit department. So I learned the importance of independent assessment in terms of balance sheets and credit worthiness of companies that Bankers Trust was looking to lend or gain an exposure to.

There were some very clever people within Bankers Trust. If you go back to that period, the two gun teams were Macquarie and BT – to work among that group of people, was incredibly influential and formative. They were heady times. A lot of money was being lent by a lot of banks and when all the banking licences opened up and the banks came in from offshore, money was very free and easy. Many Australian entrepreneurs – like Alan Bond – saw this as easy money and took the banks for a big ride. There was no division of duties, or independence, between the credit and lending departments. At most of these other places, the people who were selling the loans, and therefore earning bonuses on selling loans, were making the credit assessments as well. This inevitably ended in tears. Sorry to labour the point, but it does stick in my mind.

'The people who were selling the loans, and earning bonuses on selling loans, were making the credit assessments as well. This inevitably ended in tears.'

BK: How long did you stay with BT?

JM: I was there for about three years.

BK: So during the 1987 crash?

JM: Pretty well into the crash. The stock market was running along, and I went from auditing and insolvency to credit analysis. Looking back, it was moving me ever closer to the stock market. Of course, the stock market was absolutely on fire then, but fell very quickly at the end of 1987. So that was the point where I decided I wanted to keep moving and started on my path to funds management.

BK: Where did you go then?

JM: My initial role in funds management was at an organisation called NZI Insurance in the early part of 1988. They had an investment arm called NZI Investments and the group was exposed to a range of Kiwi and Australian entrepreneurs. In many ways, they were going through the aftermath of the market crashing. The lesson there was that we began to realise what people shouldn't do. It was pretty messy, but it was a fascinating time.

'The Kiwi entrepreneurs were going through the aftermath of the market crashing. The lesson there was that we began to realise what people shouldn't do. It was pretty messy, but it was a fascinating time.'

I've been in equities now for a long period of time, but my first role at NZI Investments was on the fixed interest side as a trainee. So I went from a qualified chartered accountant to trainee fixed interest dealer; I've still got that card. This was my introduction to funds management, and I learned a lot about fixed interest there. This role then evolved into becoming part of the equities team.

BK: What were the big lessons that you saw out of the 1987 crash?

JM: The first, in my role as an analyst, was to avoid companies with poor balance sheets and carrying too much debt. It was then reinforced at Bankers Trust through our strong independent credit disciplines, and then I saw the other side of that at NZI through some of the exposures they had taken on during the mid-80's boomtimes. So the key lesson was the strength of the balance sheet.

'Thus, identifying companies with strong balance sheets and management of integrity and who have a disciplined rule set is critical. So gaining a good sense of the integrity of people is important.'

The second thing relates to people. What I observed was that the boom times encourage unusual behaviour in people and that, in financial markets, this can lead to a lot of ill-discipline. What I learnt was that those people and organisations who steadfastly hold to a disciplined rule set, whether in boom times or bad times, will endure over the long term.

Further to that, the integrity of the individuals who are driving these is critical. Thus, identifying companies with strong balance sheets and management of integrity and who have a disciplined rule set is critical. So gaining a good sense of the integrity of people is important.

'Gaining a good sense of the integrity of people is important.'

BK: So how long did you spend at NZI?

JM: I was there for a reasonably short period, because I could see that it was in wind-down mode in the aftermath of the '87 crash. However, it did provide me with an entry into the world of funds management.

BK: You mean on the investment side?

JM: Yes, NZI Investments. The investment team had wound down – there was just myself and one other guy left running equities, and there was just one guy left in fixed interest. We learned to grow up there, but I wanted to move on and get going with my career. Sometimes you get a lucky break. For me, that happened in 1990 when I joined Perpetual as Head of Equities at age 30. That was the very early days at Perpetual; they've now grown to be one of the pre-eminent fund managers in Australia. It was a fascinating period, and in many ways, I look back on that time with considerable fondness.

'Sometimes you get a lucky break. For me, that happened in 1990 when I joined Perpetual as Head of Equities at age 30. I look back on that time with considerable fondness.'

Anton Tagliaferro, one of Australia's great investors, employed me, and I employed a guy called Peter Morgan who was my number two. In turn, we employed John Sevior and Matt Williams. Anton, myself, Pete, John and Matt were all consecutively Heads of Equity at Perpetual. I'd like to think looking back that we built something pretty good there.

BK: And enduring.

JM: Yes, something enduring, that's a very good point.

BK: So you do 10 years there before you start Perennial?

JM: I was just under five years at Perpetual, and everything was going swimmingly. At Perpetual, I was largely exposed to the financial advising network, or the retail network at that time, and then of course the institutions and the super funds were starting to emerge.

In some ways, we were the new boys on the block at Perpetual and it was exciting to be there. One of my best memories related to pitching for an institutional mandate for the very first time. We pitched for an Australian equities mandate with a large institutional fund, and we were up against all the big name incumbents – Bankers Trust and others – and somehow we managed to win it, against all the odds.

For those times, it was a big mandate; it was $50 million, and from memory it doubled up very quickly to $100 million. I've never forgotten that: we had a crack, we backed ourselves and we won it to the complete surprise of the whole industry.

BK: Why did you win that bid?

JM: I suspect they could see we were new players; they probably liked us because they could see we were hungry, we had lots to prove. I'd like to think that they saw our background, the strength of our financial analysis, and our conviction in the way we invested. Things were going well at Perpetual.

At that stage, one of the pre-eminent fund managers in Australia, was Maple-Brown Abbott, run by one of the true greats of funds management in Australia, Robert Maple-Brown. Rob sadly passed away a few years ago, and I have held always Rob in the highest esteem as an investor, as a business man, and most importantly, as an individual of the highest integrity.

Rob was looking for quite a senior person, so I received this phone call. I thought, I've got to have a look at this. The interview process seemed to go on forever. I got to the stage where I knew I wanted to join them, and Rob even offered me some equity then, which was such an opportunity, but the interview process went on for many months. That's a lesson I've learned as well – in my business, we spend a lot of time looking at people before we take them on. In the end they selected me; it was a wonderful opportunity.

BK: How long did you spend there?

JM: I was there for two years, which doesn't sound like a long time, but again, it was my call to move on. I had a senior position, was working with a pre-eminent fund manager at the time and it was all ahead of me. But I knew I wanted to do this myself. I've never wanted to die wondering; I've always believed in backing myself. I just thought, 'I've got to move on'.

'I've never wanted to die wondering; I've always believed in backing myself.'

It was such a difficult decision at the time; I've never forgotten it. I sat down with Rob and told him. It was one of the most difficult conversations I've ever had. Rob, to his eternal credit, blamed himself for me going, but it was me who made the call because in the back of my mind I wanted to back myself and do what Rob had done some time in the future.

A lot of my close friends wondered what on earth I was doing. My mother-in-law was horrified. You know, young family, three kids, I had a proper job with the best in the country. The only person that truly understood was my wife. She could see that I had this ambition to get on and have a crack and do it myself one day. It was a difficult decision to make, but a decision that had to be made.

'I had this ambition to get on and have a crack and do it myself one day.'

At that very time, fortuitously, a position came up as the Investment Director of Australian Shares at Westpac Investment Management, which at that stage was going through a major transformation, following the aftermath of the early '90s recession. Bob Joss was recruited from Wells Fargo in America, to turn Westpac around.

BK: Joss came about 1993.

JM: Yes, he'd been there for a while. It was around 1996 or thereabouts. Joss had hired Ian Macoun from Queensland Treasury Corp to turn around Westpac Investment Management.

Whilst making the decision to move on from Maple-Brown Abbott, I received a phone call for the Investment Director role and was fortunate to be chosen. It was tremendous because it put me into a very large organisation, the largest I'd worked for. Price Waterhouse and Bankers Trust in the Australian context were large, but Westpac was very big then.

I remember, at the time I joined Westpac, their Australian shares performance was towards the bottom of the tables. We improved performance and momentum was building nicely. So from a career perspective, it was very rewarding to rebuild something. However, I could see over time that I wasn't suited to working in a large organisation. So then I set up what became Perennial Value in 1999.

BK: So you're about 40 at this point?

JM: Yes, I was 39.

BK: You had a proper job, in a proper company, and you decide you're going to start Perennial Value. Big move.

JM: It was a massive move. I actually resigned from Westpac in April of 1999, before I'd set Perennial Value up. That will give you a sense of my conviction, or perhaps my naivety. The reason I resigned then was that I felt that, as I was developing my dream of building a funds management business, I would in turn not be fully focussed on looking after the best interests of my clients at Westpac. I just didn't feel good about that; it just didn't feel right.

Maintaining my integrity has always been paramount. In any people business, your integrity is all you can fall back on, so I wanted to maintain that. I remember at the time I resigned, they wanted me to stay, however I had made the call. I wasn't going to be tempted; I'd made my decision.

'Maintaining my integrity has always been paramount.'

So I said to my wife, give me till the end of year, and it went from there. I left work and was on my own. It worked out quite well, it was good timing, in a sense. I'd walk the kids up to school, and then get on with it, developing an idea into what became Perennial Value. I had an office in town with one of the stockbrokers who very kindly lent me some space to go about building up the business.

I did feel exposed at the time, but on the other hand, I was just incredibly excited. The more I looked into it, and the more people I spoke to, the more I thought the opportunity could be bigger than what I'd initially envisaged.

In a nutshell, I defined success by a little piece of paper that I no longer carry in my wallet because it's so tattered that it's at home now. It has quite a bit of sticky tape around it now because it was folded so many times in my early days when I used to look at it. It was all about where I wanted to be in five years. I wanted to have few hundred million dollars in funds under management. I wanted to take on the world that I had worked in within five years. That's how I envisaged success. I had fairly big aims at that stage. I didn't want to be a bit player; I wanted to be in the main ring.

'I didn't want to be a bit player; I wanted to be in the main ring.'

BK: What made the most difference to you getting to that point?

JM: There were a couple of things. One of the reasons I decided to do it at that stage was that I thought I could bring to bear all the experiences I'd had up until then. Our discipline is investing in Australian shares, so the first thing was to build up a very disciplined analytical framework around assessing companies. The second was building a team; that was the more critical part. I wanted to bring together a small group of people that didn't have any experience in funds management. I didn't want to bring on anyone that had any preconceived ideas of how we should invest – I wanted to start from scratch, with a new template, in terms of people. And that's what I set about doing.

One of my first employees, coincidentally, was a chartered accountant. We've a handful of chartered accountants in the team, and that's more than enough, but I wanted people with strong numbers skills. Reflecting on my interview process at Maple-Brown Abbott, we spent an awful lot of time looking at individuals, because I wanted to make sure I was bringing on the right sort of person into each role.

BK: So, in terms of selecting key people, what did you learn?

JM: In assessing candidates' CVs, people are generally unbelievably well-qualified. However, to me, it was more about assessing the individual as we built the team up. We started with a mere handful of us, and now we've a team of 15, and each interview process can go on for months. We want to understand the person.

There was one person we employed who was particularly interesting. During one of their interviews they mentioned that after work – and they were working in a large organisation, with a busy job – they'd help out in a soup kitchen in Newtown. I thought that was really interesting, so we delved into that more in

DEFINING CAREER MOMENT
- John Murray -

I think my defining business moment was deciding to go out and back myself in setting up Perennial Value.

subsequent interviews. It's all about understanding the individual. Asking those questions taught me a lot about that person. He is still with me, and still doing a fine job, but it's very much a two-way thing.

When we get to the back end of the interview process, I will say to people that it's not just about us understanding them as well as possible and making the decision that we think they're the person we'd like to take on. They've really got to want to join us as well. And that starts off for a good relationship.

BK: There are 15 support people now, and 15 investment professionals, with $5 billion under management. Was that the plan?

JM: No, it wasn't. It absolutely wasn't. It has far exceeded my expectations. I can look back and honestly say how lucky I have been. And I mean that. The more I go on in life, the more I think that most people overestimate their own abilities and underestimate the contribution of luck and timing. You've got to put yourself in a situation where luck and timing find you.

'You've got to put yourself in a situation where luck and timing find you.'

The investors that have stuck with us for many years, they understand the way we invest. I was in Melbourne last week, visiting financial advisor clients at a suburban practice. Toward the end of the meeting they said that they always enjoy talking to us because we're 'sticking to our knitting'. We just keep repeating the way we invest and the way we think about things. They said if they ever heard us change, they'd take the money from us.

BK: So how would you describe how you invest?

JM: On the surface, it's rather straightforward. Very simply, as a value investor what we're looking to do is invest in good businesses for good value. There's a margin for safety in what we do, but in looking for good businesses, there's a lot we assess.

The main one is capital preservation. That's our unofficial, number one rule. It relates to the strength of the balance sheet, essentially the mix of debt to equity. The more debt that's sitting there, the more we worry about it. That goes back to my Price Waterhouse/Bankers Trust credit analyst days.

Another key element, of course, is the integrity of management. The good value piece, where the margin for safety comes in again, is in not overpaying for a company.

BK: Are you running watch lists across many stocks to see where the value is?

JM: Absolutely. We have a range within our business – large caps, shares for income, mid caps, small caps, even micro caps more recently, which has been a very exciting initiative. We are very disciplined in terms of what we look for. For example, we run detailed models on about 250 companies, and we have some 20 to 25 years of financial history for most of them. There's a very deep financial history there.

BK: You're running a real-time view of their current values.

JM: Yes, that's right. We've got all that financial analysis there, and we've matched it up with the current share price, to come up with a current value.

BK: How does that work? Is there a team running that analysis, an investment committee that meets regularly?

JM: The team comprises analysts and portfolio managers. The portfolio managers, of which I am the senior one, make the investment decisions. The analysts undertake the fundamental research on companies, including the detailed financial modelling. This is all summarised in a stock ranking model, the Perennial Value Screen, and that becomes a key input in the stocks ultimately selected by the portfolio managers for the portfolio. Assessing management through company contact is critical too and our stock modelling is very detailed in terms of financial analysis. Sitting over the top of this process is a Portfolio Review Team, comprising the senior portfolio managers and which meets weekly. Responsibility for portfolio decisions however, ultimately rests with the portfolio managers managing their respective funds.

BK: So, in your fund, how many people work for you?

JM: There are six in total.

BK: And how does that work?

JM: We have a stock ranking model, and this ranks some 250 stocks from the best value stock to the worst value stock, and that forms the basis of what we invest in. Essentially, we want to invest in good value, good quality stocks. As they become more expensive, they move down the values rank; it's a live process. Then we sell and reinvest back into companies offering better value.

Having described the respective roles of analysts and portfolio managers, from a people perspective, what we want to do is take advantage of the collective input of everyone in that team, in order to make the best-informed investment decisions for our clients. We work on the basis that everyone in the team can bring insight to an investment decision. Right from people like myself who have been doing this for a while through to the new person who is asking questions and challenging the status quo.

Bringing people on the journey is really important. I think one of our defining features is the fact that our staff turnover is among the lowest in the industry. In our world of finance and funds management, staff turnover can be quite high.

'Bringing people on the jorney is really important... Our staff turnover is among the lowest in the industry.'

We want to attract really good people, particularly through our interview process, and retain them, and part of that is respect. I'm often staggered at the way mature adults are treated, in the workplace. We have a real mutual respect.

I set the lead early on when I started Perennial Value. If I had to go to a function at school for the kids, I went. We have a generation coming through now in their late thirties, early forties, who are all going through what I went through many years ago with young children, and I say, if they have got to go to a sausage sizzle or see their child perform – go! Don't even think about not going. I think that engenders loyalty and respect as well.

'We want to attract really good people, particularly through our interview process, and retain them, and part of that is respect.'

BK: Now let's talk returns. What sort of returns has your fund achieved over the last 17 years?

JM: Our large cap fund has delivered a return of just over 10 per cent per annum, compounded over that period of time. That's just in one of our funds. We have a range of funds. If you think about when we set up in 2000 through to now, in terms of market moves, it's been the best of all worlds and the worst of all worlds and everything in between.

BK: That large cap fund, is it top 200 companies?

JM: It's more weighted to the top 100, but it does drop down into the top 200.

BK: In terms of your 10 per cent, is that a good number, a bad number? Are you above at 5 per cent, where better than 5 per cent is a great number?

JM: We think that is a sound return over a long period of time. What most investors don't realise is that by definition, what they're doing when they invest in the stock market is that they're looking to outperform the rate of inflation. The only way you can grow your wealth is to outperform the rate of inflation. It's a fundamental rule. So I see that the stock market – and not only the Australian stock market, but also global stock markets – through a combination of dividend returns and capital growth, should outperform inflation over time.

'The only way you can grow your wealth is to outperform the rate of inflation. It's a fundamental rule.'

In simplistic terms, a 10.3 per cent per annum versus the inflation rate over the same time of 2.7 per cent – means that we've delivered a real rate of return of 7.6 per cent per annum. If you compound 6 per cent over a long time, it's a fairly significant number. I would judge that as a sound, very solid return, in terms of wealth creation over that time. However, as mentioned, we also have other share funds which have delivered sound to very strong returns for investors.

BK: This is the Shares for Income portfolio. When did you start that?

JM: In 2005. Again, its objective is to deliver a superior yield, which again, will outperform the rate of inflation. Over the 14-year period since 2005, the fund has delivered a gross yield of 8 per cent per annum, again a superior return to the rate of inflation. Gross yield is the cash dividend yield plus the franking credits added on top of that, this is effectively a pre-tax yield. And it pays monthly distributions, so investors receive a regular income stream. In their long histories, both this fund and the large cap fund have never failed to pay a distribution.

BK: Has there been capital growth in the underlying shares?

JM: There has been some capital growth on top of that, however the focus is very much on delivering a consistently strong tax effective dividend yield

BK: How large is that fund now, roughly?

JM: We have some $200 million invested in that capability. Many Australian investors still view term deposits as an income source and, whilst many investors understand the benefits of dividend income, from a long-term perspective, we are still in the early stages of the sharemarket being seen as a genuine source of income.

'From a long-term perspective, we are in the early stages of the share market being seen as a genuine source of income.'

One of the evolving trends that we want to capture is the need for growing tax-effective income in a post-retirement, ageing demographic, lower rates for longer world. So we have a big focus on income within our business, and Shares for Income will help along that way. In terms of our other share funds, our Microcap fund has been a very strong performer, having delivered a 25.7% per annum return. The smaller end of the stockmarket generally delivers stronger returns versus large caps. As a funds management business, it is important that we offer investors a select range of funds to satisfy differing needs.

BK: How is the ownership structured in the firm, and how do you use ownership to retain your key people?

JM: In short, the investment executives have majority ownership of Perennial Value and we run the business. I mentioned earlier that I think one of the key reasons we've been able to retain people is by bringing them on the journey and enhancing their careers. There are many examples of people in Perennial Value who joined us either at the start, or over ten years ago, in quite junior roles, and they have developed now to be in very senior roles.

In addition to career enhancement, the other reason we have been able to retain people is through equity. I've always been a great believer that in order to build an enduring business, and to protect and grow the business, equity ownership across the team is critical. That is the way we think. So we have spread the equity across the senior members of the team.

BK: So your key portfolio managers as well as some of your senior analysts?

JM: Over the longer term from a management succession viewpoint, you have to bring people through, and give them a lot more responsibility, and have them thinking about being owners of the business. When you're bringing people in from larger organisations to a smaller organisation, not everyone gets that, so giving them that equity ownership is important.

BK: Thank you John. We will now invite the audience to ask you some questions

Audience: Thanks for your insights, John. Can you tell us what attracts you to value investing over other strategies?

JM: The fundamental reason I'm attracted to value investing is because it works over the long term, and it makes sense. I mentioned earlier that we're looking to buy good businesses for good value, and I talked in terms of margins for safety, in terms of strength of balance sheets, and not overpaying. To me, that intuitively makes sense.

'I'm attracted to value investing because it works over the long-term, and it makes sense.'

I don't understand investors who buy good businesses that are very expensive as it means there is no margin of safety in the share price. If you own it, it can only go one way if something goes wrong. I have a very fundamental belief in that. Over the last few years, value investing has been very much out of favour, so it hasn't been much fun, to be frank, to be a value investor.

But we turn up every day of the week absolutely convinced that that's what works, over the long term. In looking for value, we have often assessing companies whose share prices have fallen and have overreacted to some temporary bad news. We're over here looking at the unfavoured companies. There aren't often too many people at that party, which makes us a contrarian investor.

When you're running against the pack – not just in investing, but in life – it can be a very uncomfortable place to be. But I like people who are contrarians. I look for that characteristic in the people in our team.

Audience: How long did it take for you to feel the business was successful, and what kept you going until that point? I'm sure it wasn't all good times.

JM: I set myself five years and success came to us a little sooner than we'd anticipated, but it was all or nothing. There was no plan B, which was a good thing because it kept me focused.

Part of your question relates to the tough moments. Yes, at the moment, it's tough particularly as value investing has been very much out of favour, and the industry right now is more challenging than it's ever been, there's no doubt about that. But we're up for the fight, and we have invested in newer capabilities, such as microcaps, to meet investors changing demands.

There are a few things that carry you through, and the first is resilience. I'm a massive believer in resilience. Secondly, just turning up every day of the week. There's nothing like turning up every day of the week. In your darkest moment, just keep turning up. There could be an opportunity just around the corner, and if you don't turn up, you won't see that.

'In your darkest moment, just keep turning up. There could be an opportunity just around the corner, and if you don't turn up, you won't see it.'

The only other point I would make, which I should have highlighted, is that we have a very strong mantra of clients first. That's all that matters in a service industry. If we're not delivering to our clients' expectations, we don't deserve to be there.

If your people are focused on clients-first from day one it can make a big difference, and that can very much help you during those tougher, more challenging periods as well.

This interview was conducted live, as part of the Kelly+Partners Next Generation Education+Thought Leadership Program series of speaking events.

INVESTMENT WISDOM LESSONS

• Have the courage

of your convictions, as your best ideas will invariably be contrary to popular thinking.

• Be careful

to distinguish between investing and speculating.

• Develop

a rigorous methodology which can be consistently applied across all of your investment ideas.

David Paradice

Managing Director, Paradice Investment Management

'There's no better fertiliser than the owner's footsteps.'

David Paradice founded Paradice Investment Management
in 1999. Paradice Investment Management invests in equities
around the world with offices in Australia and the USA.
It is a privately owned company with a team of 43 people, with
approximately $16.6 billion funds under management.
David supports charities across a number of fields including
humanitarian, the arts, environmental, and education.
He is chairman of the Taronga Zoo Conservation Society because
of its environmental work, especially in the oceans.
David currently sits on the board of The Future Generation
Investment Fund, a LIC that donates their management fees
back to children's charities. He also assisted in setting up the
Clean Energy Finance Corporation.
In 2017 he was awarded an AO for distinguished service to the
community through philanthropic contributions and charitable
support, and to business and commerce in the field
of investment management.
http://paradice.com

Interview

BRETT KELLY: If there was a motto or a quote or thought that best summarised your approach to life or investing, what would it be?

DAVID PARADICE: Always do the right thing and not what you can get away with. When I first started, I spoke to Robert Maple-Brown, he's from Maple-Brown Abbott. He's a really nice guy and our industry is a tough industry and there are a lot of guys who take shortcuts. And as with anything, it just doesn't work taking shortcuts. And Robert showed me that good guys can make a go of it and he didn't compromise on integrity and authenticity. For me, that's really important.

BK: What was your background? Did you grow up in Sydney?

DP: I grew up in Scone, in the Hunter Valley. My father was a doctor and my mother was a teacher. I was one of six, and I'm in the middle. I used to spend a lot of time outdoors because we grew up in a small farm of 150 acres, so I used to do a lot of outside stuff, I wasn't inside a lot. My mother used to have an interest in the stock market and I always liked to be very exposed to the speed bumps of life, so I don't mind backing myself.

I remember back in 1984, I was in London selling sandwiches and it was good, because if I'd sell more sandwiches, the more money I'd make and if I didn't sell any, then I wouldn't earn anything. As opposed to working in an organisation where you're paid a salary and then someone else decides your bonus. I don't mind taking the risk of being very performance-orientated, and our business is built around being performance orientated. My number one focus is delivering performance for clients. There have been no situations where I could've taken a shortcut, or I could've done something to get away with something which was financially right for us but was not right for the clients. We never do that because it's just not the right thing to do.

'There have been no situations where I could've taken a shortcut, or I could've done something to get away with something which was financially right for us but was not right for the clients. We never do that because it's just not the right thing to do.'

BK: Where do you think that mindset came from, this 'Back yourself'? Because doing the right thing speaks to a person's character. Where is that from?

DP: I don't know.

BK: Is it the big family?

DP: No, I don't know because none of the others had...

BK: Had that mindset?

DP: No, my youngest brother probably has it. He's a stockbroker but none of the others have really gone down this route. That's not to say they wouldn't back themselves, but I actually don't know. My father's not very commercial, he's a doctor, and my mum's not really commercial.

BK: What did you study at university?

DP: Commerce at the University of New South Wales.

BK: Did you find that that training helped you?

DP: I think it was hard; I didn't do that well. I got through the three years and I think I only failed one subject, but I didn't get high distinctions and that kind of stuff, so I'm not that smart [chuckles]. What I do understand is – I try to focus on people and understanding what makes people work. And I'm happy to share things with my colleagues. There are other people that take the other option and concentrate, say, for example, on ownership of the business. But for me, it's not about being the wealthiest guy in the graveyard, it's about doing the right thing by the clients and all stakeholders including staff. So we've shared the ownership of this business amongst a lot of the staff as opposed to having it concentrated with me.

'For me, it's not about being the wealthiest guy in the graveyard, it's about doing the right thing by the clients and all stakeholders, including staff.'

BK: How long have you been running the company? When did you start it?

DP: We got the first money on 6 March 2000. So, on 6 March 2020 it'll be 20 years.

BK: What was the founding vision of the business?

DP: I really didn't have a plan. I was a stock picker for five or six years and I had these unbelievably good numbers. But the company was quite big and I just wanted to have a go myself. I enjoy accountability and leading by performance. This business has grown up on accountability and delegation of authority and giving people empowerment.

'I just wanted to have a go myself. I enjoy accountability and leading by performance.'

There are so many other companies where people work with say, a fund manager at the top and they provide ideas. What we do here is each of the fund managers has influence on the portfolio. People like Capital or Fidelity have analysts all over the world that provide things, and fund managers. But for me, a fund manager needs to be in touch with the company. So, all of our guys, all of our fund managers go and see all the companies themselves and make decisions themselves.

BK: So when you started did you start with a mentality that you'd have broadly based ownership, that you would have portfolio managers in touch with companies? Was there a bit of a playbook that you had in mind?

DP: Yes, I did. So, people have to be generalists, to look at any investment over Australia. There are points in time when property will be better placed by retailing companies, or technology will be better, or commodities will be better. So, you need someone to be able to look at every investment. As soon as you start going – and this has happened to me, where you employ someone and they're a specialist in media... I saw a guy, a competing fund manager employ a guy from media, his portfolio started drifting into media free-to-air and they just got belted, so you can't have that.

So, they need to be generalists. They need to be people that are focused on absolute returns and not financial engineering. When you're running large cap money you have to be conscious of what's in the index but you do want to have an absolute return kind of mindset. Because at the end of the day, they always say that you can't bank relative performance. It helps to focus on risk on the downside. You don't want to go and buy a company which is large in the index but it's really poor quality and it's really expensive because there's downside risk associated with it.

BK: So, you start, you've got this idea of a funds management business. Was it going to be small caps, large caps, lots of money, a little bit of money?

DP: So, we took $200 million. I got $30 million on 6 March 2000, and then in the first year we raised $200 million. Then in 2014 we basically turned from $200 odd million to $2.2 billion and we were too big for the index. We ended up handing back $800 million and that was because at the end of the day our focus is always on the outcome for clients. Financially, it wasn't a good decision to make, but for the clients, the existing clients, we took money across all the clients and redeemed individual ones. Their remaining money benefited from performance because we reduced the small cap money.

BK: And what was the money? Was it family office money, institutional money?

DP: Institutional money.

BK: And the first $30 million?

DP: It was raised through our employee's superannuation trust, and then various industry funds have been supporters since then. All of our funds have done well over a long period of time, and each of those funds have allowed us to grow.

BK: So just going back to you wanting generalists, wanting absolute return, wanting people that act in the interest of the clients. When you're really looking at people, what makes a great fund manager or investor or stock picker?

DP: Someone who's focused in on the earnings, the earnings of the company and the fundamentals of the company. Someone who loves how businesses operate. I find myself, wherever I am, on holidays and I'm in a shop and there are lots of people and families coming in asking about prices. I just love all that stuff and everybody else here loves it.

'Someone who's focused in on the earnings, the earnings of the company and the fundamentals of the company. Someone who loves how businesses operate. I find myself, wherever I am, on holidays and I'm in a shop and there are lots of people and families coming in asking about prices. I just love all that stuff and everybody else here loves it.'

DP: I've spoken to guys who are very ordinary fund managers and they're talking to me about the weight of money, wanting to buy a particular stock and pushing a stock up and all that kind of crap. That's bullshit. It's unrelated to the fundamentals of a business. So it's focusing a lot on fundamentals of business and still talking about businesses as opposed to charting. They could be right and that's all weight of money and where things are flying, but at the end of the day, an ability to tell someone whether they're telling the truth or not is important for us.

BK: When you say you're a stock picker, what do you say a stock picker is and what's your process?

DP: So in other words, it's going out and seeing companies, coming back, doing modelling work and looking at the numbers and understanding what are the principal drivers of a particular stock. It's looking for the production of free cash flow and looking for a building to be able to fund growth and the ability to be able to have incremental return on invested capital. That needs to keep on growing because it ultimately leads to increased earnings and increased dividends per share, which is the long-term driver of value.

It's funny, you know, over the years you look at various investments and I remember looking at one of these companies years and years ago, and I could see, and there's lots of them, but this is a really old example, where Queensland TAB got affected by the weather, they went and bought the South Australian TAB. They had all the costs and with technology evolving and evolving but they were able to put the revenue of South Australian TAB under the Queensland TAB and get rid of the costs and become less vulnerable to the weather.

BK: They put the Head Co costs across bigger business?

DP: Yes, and all the things that come with that.

BK: Same business, not a new adventure.

DP: Yes, and I thought over time those dividends are going to keep going, but they're so reliable that in time people will see this as a bond, an annuity. And it was massive.

BK: In terms of models, spread over time.

DP: Yeah, so the keys in small caps or any company is obviously if you look at earnings growth and PE expansion. I don't mind buying that contrarian type stuff. You might have situations where you've got a business with a broken-down division which is an evaluation of a company, like the negative earnings. You get rid of that division, close it down, turn around, it has a bigger impact.

BK: Big step change, yes.

DP: That only comes from visiting companies.

BK: Actually asking those questions.

DP: Yes, and talking about growth.

BK: So, sometimes bad news is not bad news.

DP: That's right.

BK: Unless they're not going to do anything about it.

DP: That's right, and it all depends. The mistakes that we've made have been selling the really good companies, well-run companies way too early. The well-run companies just continue to find out ways of being able to manage their way through cycles, and there's always challenges.

'The mistakes that we've made have been selling the really good companies, well-run companies way too early.'

BK: Do you think that's because people believe that there are more very good companies than there really are, or more excellent management teams than there really are?

DP: Well, companies get too expensive sometimes, but then they've got management, there'll be a stabilisation. There's price and they look at it, and it's really expensive and then the earnings come through. I mean, I don't know anything about CSL, but CSL probably would look too expensive.

BK: It's a pretty well-run business.

DP: But even Reece, you know, I haven't really followed it recently but Reece is just a plumbing supply business. But the management, the Wilsons, that are involved run it really well. There's ARB, which is just a bull bar business. They're pretty basic businesses but they're run by good guys. Even Premier Investments which they've just changed. It's Solly Lew. It's just from all of the work.

BK: So, when I look at those guys, I think these are people that love business. My experience often is that they don't think about much else because that's what they love thinking about. It's a bit like backing or betting against champions. It's a bit of a fool's endeavour in that those two look like they're probably going to be able to run retail business as well as anyone.

DP: And they have total focus. I was on an aeroplane, I landed at about say, 7:30 on a Friday night. I was going back home and one of Just Jeans' people who was flying backwards and forwards from Melbourne was going home in a car and she said, 'Would you like a lift?'. Anyway, Solly [Solomon Lew] rings up and says, at 8 o'clock on a Friday night, 'How was the week, how was the day, how's sales going?' And they say there's no better fertiliser than the owner's footsteps.

There's no better fertiliser than the owner's footsteps.'

BK: Yeah, that's a great saying.

DP: Whatever Solly's doing, he's onto it. He's a really good operator.

BK: Very interesting.

DP: You can't get away from people. We're challenged at the moment by computers but hopefully, it becomes more about the human touch over the computers.

BK: Do you think that really excellent management is very important in terms of relative performance versus the industry versus other options?

DP: Oh, absolutely. It's like Warren Buffett says – what does he say? Buying a...

BK: Buying a great business that can be run by a fool because one day a fool will run it.

DP: I totally agree with that. It's just a case for anyone that has a business. Technology changes the dynamics of, or is changing the dynamics of, all the industries. If you can get a business which can evolve with those changing dynamics and is well-run, that's a great recipe for success.

BK: What do you see in the structure of your business?

DP: It's privately held and the equity is shared amongst everyone.

BK: Just portfolio managers or your admin, everyone?

DP: The admin guys, too. And after people have been here for a period of time.

*'The mistakes
that we've made
have been selling
the really good
companies, well-run
companies way
too early.'*

BK: How long do they have to be in the business?

DP: Three years is the set rule. But it is the inclusion of those guys as owners of the equity which helps manage the business.

BK: How many people are there now?

DP: 50.

BK: And what are the total funds managed?

DP: $17 billion.

BK: Is size an issue for the business or an issue for a fund? Buffett talks about size being a barrier to performance, but are you structuring to manage the that issue?

DP: It is, but we have limited growth in a number of these businesses where we still have lots of capacity to grow. So, although you're on $12 billion in Australia, so these are the Australian funds, and this is actually June, it's now the end of September, so it's a bit old.

BK: Do you think that by limiting the size of these funds, you prevent the sizes from becoming a barrier to performance?

DP: That's right. Because they're all run by separate teams, they're focused on those little amounts of money. If you gave $12 billion to some fund manager to run nowadays, he would have a bigger waiting in large cap stocks, I suppose, and a tiny bit in the mid and smalls.

BK: But you guys started from small to large. Is that how you brief the business?

DP: Yes, and that I think has had an effect on the culture of the place. Small cap guys are very focused on stock selection kind of absolute returns, and they focus on absolute turns because there's like 12, 13 hundred stocks in the index and maybe the biggest one is 1 per cent or 0.5 per cent. So, we focus on having about 50 odd stocks, 60 odd stocks, so you really don't buy things relative to the index. What's happening now with computers is that the fund managers delivering these returns just don't get paid. We don't get paid for them. Their returns actually have been a lot better recently because you get things like, for example, here everybody's buying all the bank stocks, technology stocks and the big value. So, you get this situation where a lot of active managers are underperforming at the moment but I'm praying that rationale might come back and fundamental earnings will be important.

BK: Let's talk about that. That's really interesting. We look at zero interest rates, zero bond rates, potentially negative interest rates. I read an article the other day about what happens if they just keep printing money forever? What, in your view, drives the market back to fundamentals? This article was arguing that capitalism is being replaced with a form of statism where the state just washes the economy with money and so there's no consequence of underperformance, ultimately. What happens?

DP: I don't know how it unwinds. The negative interest rate environment is concerning. You look at what happened in Japan – it's a bit different over there, but the equity market and probably prices are probably lower now than what they were 30 years ago so it hasn't been performing well. I do see the market continue to go up. Some of these larger technology companies are trading at reasonable multiples, but of course with technology there are barriers to entry, there's the first mover advantage.

But just like Telstra had leading market share in telecommunications and they were big in mobile, after a while people just started nipping away at the edges and they have to reduce their pricing. If they can't, their price and the business goes through a discounted valuation. People were saying that, in time, with the big guys in America that have benefited from the cloud, there'd be other people competing for that cloud space. So, with interest rates though where they are, it has an effect on the valuation that people pay for stocks. So, if interest rates are 1 per cent then...

BK: Rates are very low and there are discounts...

DP: Yes, and then people inverse that and they say, 'Oh, well, they should be trading at 100 times'. Well, there's a problem with that because it can be 100 times. Firstly, they've got to get the growth to justify that. But if the economy starts turning around or whatever, the interest rates start moving up, it's a real problem for those higher and really expensive stocks because there's no margin for error, ever. Like you said, they probably have to go and keep printing money and that will continue to drive stuff, but as an investor you don't want to change your style. The downside of protection for us is important. Going into high risk is not...

BK: Why people invest with you?

DP: Yes, so style drift is a really important thing. Some of these, they call 'quality growth'. It's interesting, I mean, everybody's trying to get quality growth.

BK: A bit of word games, right?

DP: To tell you the truth, I don't know.

BK: But if you stick to a deep value style, is it your view that other than potential outflows, if people move money to things that they find more sexy?

DP: I don't know whether we're deep value. Like I say, you kind of guard. We will buy expensive stuff if it's growing. But people have these portfolios where their PEs are trading way above the market and they call it quality premium. Whereas that might be another word of saying how expensive your portfolio is compared to the market. Back in 2000 there were a lot of Australian technology companies that were going up through the roof.

BK: And they were the leaders, they weren't just the rubbish. The rubbish went up, too, but the leading in each category was right up there.

DP: But you have got things like Seek and Car Sales.

BK: Real businesses.

DP: Like open telecommunications and numerous standalone companies back in 2000. They had a rough crop because the guys in America that are looking over here are saying, 'Hey, hang on, I might go down there. They made so much money on their IT platform, let's just go and do a bit of advertising and put one out.' That's why Australia's ability to compete in tech is generally high. You get the Atlassian guys and a few outliers but generally I think it's tough.

BK: Why are you guys in San Francisco and Denver?

DP: I employed a guy 10 years ago to run our global all cap and he lived in Denver.

BK: So, talent driven.

DP: Talent driven, same with San Francisco. They're actually very good time zones for running global because, obviously, you've got England and Europe in the morning and Asia in the afternoon.

BK: If you could tell your younger self something that you know now that you wish you knew then, what would that be?

DP: Well, there's probably lots of things. You can't go back and rewrite history on facts, so this is more a philosophical thing.

BK: Yeah, like you mentioned you backed yourself. Would you have backed yourself harder, would you backed yourself earlier if you knew about the full benefit in your capacity to execute?

'One of the things
about investing is
that if you make
any mistakes, just
sell it and move on.
It doesn't matter
when you bought
the stocks.'

DP: No, I think I probably would not try and take the speed bumps so hard. Every time we underperform or whatever it is, I take it hard. But, if you don't take it hard, do you end up taking it harder?

BK: Does it make you softer if you aren't hard on yourself?

DP: I love being able to generate good performance for clients, that's my big thing. I'm not great with conflict. So, I probably should've addressed some internal issues with people earlier. If you make a mistake you should always get rid of them sooner rather than later.

BK: Do it early.

DP: I'm hopeless at that kind of thing.

BK: It's hard. It's very hard.

DP: I'm much more of a marketer. I'm a chatty sales guy rather than hard-assed business guy.

BK: Do you have any biggest regrets in terms of investing mistakes?

DP: I haven't done any investing myself for a while, I've delegated it all out to various people. Delegation is an important thing to do. It goes back to the old days of stocks, we've given too much of the benefit of the doubt to companies and then they just continue to disappoint us. And that's a big thing … It's giving the benefit.

I've made lots and lots of errors of listening to people. One of the things about investing is that if you make any mistakes, just sell it and move on. It doesn't matter when you've done it. It doesn't matter when you bought the stocks. See, some people buy a stock one day and they're embarrassed about selling it. But if you make a mistake you need to do it straight away.

BK: So, don't get invested in your mistake.

DP: Yes and a lot of people do. I used to have the problem of doing that myself. It's really about investing and learning your mistakes and it's just like they talk about the rose garden, Warren Buffett at the rose garden. You don't leave your flowers sitting in the rose garden. You sell them, you prune out the roses and then keep going.

BK: But the professionals, typically when they prune – a good example I use is whenever the gardener comes to prune your garden, it looks like they've

killed the plant. Whereas whenever non-professionals do it, we fiddle at the edges whereas they just come in and...

DP: Yes, I know.

BK: There's a bit of a lesson in there. Yhe professional pruner versus the amateur.

DP: I do labour on a lot of stuff. I do labour on a lot of key stuff.

BK: Final question, work-life balance. You're running a big business, you're running people, a huge amount of responsibility. How do you have time for your family, have time for your health and just manage your life?

DP: It's a massive thing and I make an effort to spend time, as much time as I can with my family and it's really important for me to do that. And so, I always make sure I'm always there at major school events or, you know, there for the holidays. So, it's probably the most important thing for me.

BK: How do you switch off?

DP: I play polo badly. Which I'm glad about, because if I could play it well then I probably wouldn't be doing what I am now. I do like polo because you're on the horse and you can't think of anything else but what's happening in front of you and it's really good for the mind. It gives me a relief and you can't think of anything else while playing.

I like sport and I love exercise and being outside. I rode a mountain bike, for example, with my son from New Mexico to Canada, which was particularly hard. It was 38 days over 4,400km. Mountain biking is similar to polo because you can't get on the phone and you can't talk and you need to focus. I also like going for runs. I was swimming this morning in 16C down at Bondi Beach at 5:30. I love starting really early. I love getting to the office early.

BK: What time do you normally get here?

DP: About 6:30am, 6:45am.

BK: Why is that?

DP: Just because it's nice. Beautiful time of the day and get a lot done.

BK: Thank you very much for your time.

INVESTMENT WISDOM LESSONS

• Right always wins

Always do the right thing and not what
you can get away with.

• Stay calm

Don't follow the herd and don't lose your
head when everybody else is losing theirs.

• Face facts

Rely on fundamentals and not emotions.

Joseph Skrzynski

Co-Chairman, Castle Harlan Australian Mezzanine Partners (CHAMP)

'Australia is a meritocracy; if you've got a good idea you can really do something with it.'

Joseph Skrzynski is Co-Chairman of CHAMP's Investment Committee. He is a founding partner of CHAMP Private Equity and its predecessor, Australian Mezzanine Investments (AMIL), which he co-founded with Bill Ferris in 1987. He has held numerous portfolio company directorships since this time, including publicly listed company directorships in Australia and Asia on behalf of both the AMIL and CHAMP Funds.

Joseph has been active in the Australian Private Equity and Venture Capital Association Limited (AVCAL), including time as president. His contribution to the industry has been honoured with the inaugural Asian Adventure Capital Journal Lifetime Achievement Award in 2008 and the inaugural Australian Venture Capital Association Limited Lifetime Contribution Award in 2008, which were both shared jointly with Bill Ferris.

He has also been active in community affairs for over 40 years and is currently a member of the international boards of Human Rights Watch, The Conversation Media Group is a director of Philanthropy Australia and The Observership Program, and chairs his family philanthropic foundation, The Sky Foundation. Joseph graduated with honours from the Faculty of Economics, University of Sydney in 1969, was made a Member of the Order of Australia in 1993, and in 2008 became an Officer in the Order of Australia for services to the industry and philanthropy.

https://cpecapital.com

Interview

BRETT KELLY: Joseph, I always start with this question: if there was a motto, quote or thought that best summarises your approach to life, what would it be?

JOSEPH SKRZYNSKI: Ultimately, it's about values; in everything you do. Values and the people you work with. I think that comes from my parents, particularly my father, and his experience in War World II of having been taken to a concentration camp for two and a half years which he survived.

BK: Was that in Poland?

JS: Yes, we're Polish, originally. My father was part of the political round-up when the Nazis were getting rid of the leadership class. He observed that it wasn't the strongest people in the camp that made it through; it was those who were able to mentally – more than physically – handle the situation. It was about having the mental capacity to make sense of where you were and keep going against impossible odds. That was always an inspiration to me – how you think about things is most important.

'How you think about things is most important.'

In my father's case, in the camp he dedicated himself to the Virgin Mary, and then wrote a wonderful book on the subject when he retired called, controversially for a Catholic, *Mary the Jewess, Mother of Christ.*

The other thing that came from my father's experience was clarity about what to value in life. His family were very wealthy before the war; there was a lot of inherited wealth in property, just east of Krakow. After the war the communists confiscated their home, which subsequently became a school for 200 boarding students, so it was quite large – but I was hearing these stories in a one-bedroom flat in Rose Bay where we rented out the bedroom as recently arrived refugees who had lost everything in the war and the Russian occupation.

My parents' ability to not spend their life complaining about what they'd lost, but instead get on with their life, was inspiring. The knowledge that material possessions can be ephemeral was important – I realised that if you build your life and your self-esteem around what you own, it's a pretty deceptive and fragile environment to live in.

'My parents' ability to not spend their life complaining about what they'd lost, but instead get on with their life, was inspiring.'

BK: Your dad came to Australia in 1950 after World War II. What was his training?

JS: Mum and Dad were both law graduates from the University of Warsaw. Dad went on to do higher studies in diplomacy and international relations in Vienna before returning to Poland at the outbreak of the war; they were both from educated backgrounds.

BK: Do you know what your father's background was?

JS: My dad's father was in the diplomatic corps. We had a relation, Count Alexander Skrzynski, who was foreign minister of Poland and briefly, prime minister of Poland. The family tree goes back to 1100, so there's a sense of history in the family. Then you get the total upheaval of being stripped of everything and in a concentration camp, and then after being rescued by the Americans in migrant camps in Germany after the war. My father smuggled my mother out of communist Poland to join him in Germany.

'My father smuggled my mother out of communist Poland to join him in Germany.'

I had the wonderful experience of retelling this story when I was chairman of the Sydney Opera House. My secretary got a phone call from the Minister for Citizenship, under the Howard government, when they were escalating the importance of citizenship ceremonies for people who'd come through the "right door". I was able to tell how it's been wonderful for me as a migrant to rise to such a position. I never thought I'd become something like chairman of the Sydney Opera House – when I arrived in Australia, I couldn't speak English. I recounted how none of it would have been possible except for people smugglers – my mother had been smuggled out of Poland into East Germany, then into West Berlin, and with the help of the American army, from West Berlin to West Germany.

The minister was not amused, of course, but a few months later, when my wife was involved in trying to get recognised asylum seekers out of Villawood Detention Camp, I wrote to him. There was a Syrian Christian who'd been in there for five years, an old man, and the Catholic church said they'd look after him. I wrote a letter to the Minister of Citizenship and in reply got a one-liner saying it was a matter for the Minster for Immigration.

Three months later I got another one-liner from him saying that the man had got his residency. It's a good example of change not being about statistics and ideology; when you're talking about matters of policy and public interest, it's personal stories that actually reach people.

'When you're talking about matters of policy and public interest, it's personal stories that actually reach people.'

BK: You mention your father dedicated himself to the Virgin Mary, how significant was this for him?

JS: Without faith, you can become depressed; that's a slippery slope. In the concentration camp, the knife edge equation of calories in, calories out meant that if you didn't look after yourself, if you didn't wash, you got dysentery and were gone. He maintained that discipline because he was convinced he was going to get through it. He also ran into an old friend that used to work for him on his estate who clued him up on woodwork, so he was able to get his work assignment inside a furniture factory when he was in Sachsenhausen camp. The factory had the benefit of a fire, which kept the glue melted. That was a lot better than being out in the snow digging up beetroot. It was the combination of keeping mentally stable and then being artful enough to get into the right type of work that helped him survive. He says he couldn't have done it without faith.

BK: Your parents came to Australia penniless, but rich in their values and spiritual life. What else did they pass on to you?

JS: My father, unable to replicate the culture of Europe that he was used to – the art galleries, the operas, the museums – adapted himself to Australia's beautiful unspoilt nature. I remember being taken on long bush walks; my father became an absolute expert on trees and birds from travelling up and down the country. He looked for the best of what this new country had to offer rather than trying to replicate the old. He taught me not to hold on to things and to instead look for what's best in where you find yourself.

'My father taught me not to hold on to things and to instead look for what's best in where you find yourself.'

There was also the world of ideas, history, music and literature and so on; there were always discussions around the table between my parents and the friends they made, among them artists.

BK: After school, what did you study?

JS: I was good at debating at school, so I thought I might do law, but my parents talked me out of it. For them, law was a codification of the social mores and rules of a particular society, their Polish legal degrees were useless in Australia so they advised me to do something international.

In the end I did an economics degree with honours in accounting at the University of Sydney. I thought it would be useful and not too limiting later on. We had a revolutionary teacher called Professor Chambers and the course was an insight into business thinking, which was absolutely brilliant. It focused on the gulf between statutory accounts and the information business executives actually used to run business.

That was the most useful part of what I studied in a formal sense, but the other most useful part was actually being involved in student politics during the Vietnam era (1966-69). There was a lot going on at that time; there was the sexual revolution, drugs were coming on to the scene, marijuana. There were student revolts and students demanding representation on the decision-making bodies at university. The Vietnam War was a big thing. There were changes everywhere – what you wore, what you drank and ate; everything.

I ended up being the vice president and treasurer of the Student Representative Council (SRC). Jim Spiegelman was president and there many others like Michael Kirby, Geoffrey Robertson, Alan Cameron, radical in their youth, and later leaders in society. As treasurer, I was required to have cash on hand to bail people out during the Vietnam demonstrations.

The banks closed at three, but the demos didn't start till five, and you had to have cash; the police didn't take credit cards or cheques. I got to know the head of the riot squad, Freddy Longbottom, and got into the habit of ringing him at about 2.30pm to get a quote on how much money I was going to need that afternoon.

When I got to know him better, I asked him how it all worked. He said that if the boss, who was Robert Askin, the Premier at the time, had a bad time in Question Time, Fred would get a phone call to say they needed law and order on the front page the following day, so he knew they had to make a lot of arrests.

BK: You would need a lot of money then.

JS: Yes. It was pretty interesting at 18 to see society at work: you had the politicians telling the police what to do, the students organising, the police organising both sides leaking tips to mates in the media. It was a great education in which way was up. I had the university karate club for my bodyguards, as I had up to $20,000 in cash at times.

BK: Did you have any sort of vision of what you might do after university?

JS: I didn't have a clear vision of a career path, but after my involvement in the student community I knew it would not be just a narrow professional career. Then through an artist friend of my father, I was introduced to Sir Paul Strasser, a very successful businessman, a Hungarian.

He interviewed me, but it was more like an IQ test. He asked me if he hired me, how much would he pay me; how would he make money out of paying me that amount; and what would it benefit him. It was a very interesting interview.

BK: What was he doing at that point?

JS: He was very successful in real estate. He was, for his time, like a Lowy or a Gandel figure. Every Hungarian in Sydney with a business idea was hitting on him for finance. So he put me onto the deals he'd agreed to do. They weren't real estate deals, they were actually private equity and venture capital. They were start-ups; Hungarians with a good idea for a business.

BK: I imagine that was good experience because your investor is an actual person; you can see the money going from the actual person into an actual business.

JS: Absolutely. The investment was on his balance sheet, on his business partners' balance sheet. With his supervision – and from the way he decided which deals to go into, what was important in monitoring them, and how to assess ideas and people – I learned the ropes. Strasser's number one rule was: never invest with people you don't trust. It doesn't matter how smart you are, they've got 24 hours a day to figure out how to diddle you, you might devote an hour a day. They're going to win.

'Never invest with people you don't trust.
It doesn't matter how smart you are.'

It was an early lesson in not getting swept up with an idea; rather always make sure that the person you're going to back is an honest person and capable of executing on the plan – have they got the experience to do what they say they can do? And if it grows to a scale, what else are they going to need around them for it to continue to be successful.

BK: How was Strasser investing? Was he looking for a quick turn in a capital gain?

JS: No, it wasn't quick. They were good ideas that were being built, good businesses that were all going to be valuable one way or another. It was about the opportunity to build a business.

BK: So was he looking for majority stakes, minority stakes?

JS: It was a bit of everything: they were 50-50 or sometimes a minority. We also got involved in some management buyouts as well. It became known that we were doing private investment, so other people started coming to us. Bill was doing a bit of that when he came back from Harvard.

We had come across each other at university, but he was a few years ahead of me. Then we crossed paths again when we were both doing what was essentially private equity back in the early 1970s. I did a couple of management buyouts with Ron Brierley and Industrial Equity. Another one that was terrific was Ford Sherington. Every kid had a Globite school bag in those days, a brown fibre board bag – that was made by Ford Sherington.

Ford Sherington sat on a large piece of property out in the western suburbs in Sydney. That property was ripe for redevelopment as housing, but it was a factory in the early 1970s making the Globite bags but also more interestingly the first baby car capsule seats. That's the business we ended up holding on to and developing; it was terrific.

BK: So, you bought Ford Sherington's business?

JS: Yes. We did privatise the company. We sold off the land, transferred the bag manufacture as it was too expensive and focused on the new product, the baby seat.

BK: And did you do that with Bill?

JS: No, that was under Strasser – with Strasser's money – and John Hunt, the entrepreneur who brought the idea to us. We validated it and used the real-estate experience of Strasser's group; he was able to handle the property side of it. John and I concentrated on building up the baby seat side of the business.

BK: Was that eventually sold?

JS: It was, eventually in a trade sale, yes for a very profitable outcome. We had a portfolio of other successful investments, including hospitality, and industrial chemicals. That was all good fun until interest rates went up to 17 per cent in the late 1970s. I remember Paul Strasser taking me to bank meetings earlier on where young bankers from the National Australia Bank were offering to lend 110 per cent of valuation on property deals in Strasser's property division just to get money out the door and get their bonuses.

Strasser embarked on a long-term land bank strategy, but when interest rates exploded to over 17 per cent, the holding costs made it unviable. The National Bank put in administrators on the whole conglomerate of companies. Our section, which wasn't in real estate and wasn't heavily indebted, had to be folded in because it was a private company and everything was cross-collateralised. I stayed on for a year under the administrator. I learned more in that year than in many other years. When things are a success, no-one is exactly sure what worked so everybody takes credit, but when things hit the wall, you really see how banks work in terms of their securities; you see how partners work when they try and scramble out; you see where the cracks appear.

No-one should be allowed to go too far into business without going through some sort of catastrophe to really take stock of what really works and what doesn't in relationships, in contracts, in finance. That was enormously helpful for me. Then I got offered other jobs out of there.

'When things hit the wall, you really see how banks work in terms of their securities; you see how partners work when they try and scramble out; you see where the cracks appear.'

BK: So it's the late '70s, you're 25, 26, and you'd been a company director for four or five years.

JS: Yes, Strasser put me on the boards of the companies that he invested in, so it was very early in terms of my experience. It was an apprenticeship with a really good business brain, but in terms of actually running the investments for him, I was definitely in the deep end.

BK: Did Strasser survive that?

JS: He did, in the sense that he had other assets that weren't part of the real estate group that the bank took charge of. For me, it was about human nature and how people react when there's a strain and a stress, and how banks and lawyers and what documents really mean when push comes to shove.

People sign up to all sorts of things when money is flowing, but then when times get tough, you need to understand how banks react and how enforcement is carried out. We had some great success in businesses that we developed, but watching how a major empire gets pulled apart was a terrific experience for me.

From then, I was invited to join Bob Selden at Pittsburgh National Selden, a boutique investment bank specialising in advisory services to large private companies, cooperatives. We had done work with them on some of our Strasser deals. It was focused on debt, and mergers and acquisitions. I did that type work for about three years before joining the Australian Film Commission as chief executive.

It was a bit of a lateral move, but I'd kept in touch with friends from when I was treasurer at university, people I had funded in the cultural clubs who turned out to be artists and filmmakers. Since university I'd given them some advice on the side and raised finance for *My Brilliant Career*, for Margaret Fink, worked with Pat Lovell on *Gallipoli* and a few other films. They put my name up to the Film Commission and I thought it would be interesting, so took a three-year contract.

It was like venture capital on an industry scale – the industry was using government money to kickstart the local TV and film production industry. It was a fascinating time 1979 to 1981; things were starting to take off and it was great getting to know some of the wonderful filmmakers like George Miller and Gillian Armstrong.

'It was like venture capital on an industry scale – the industry was using government money to kickstart the local TV and film production industry.'

The world was waking up to a new Australian style of storytelling a film. I was going to film markets and festivals around the world, meeting the Warner Brothers people and others – it was an amazing time. We had a budget of $4 million for all the filmmaking in Australia, which had kept the lid on budgets. Feature films were being made for between $300 000 and $500 000 each and filmmakers had to take it in turns to get government grants. The problem was, our directors were starting to become internationally successful and we were going to lose them overseas if we couldn't increase the budgets. The trick was getting the money up. I was lucky to have an opportunity through the minister at the time, Bob Ellicott, to put up a new idea to government, which was a tax-deduction for encouraging private involvement in film.

The challenge was getting a deduction upfront as at the time the tax profile of film investment was a 21-year depreciation schedule, whereas within two years you knew the financial outcome and if in loss, you had to wait 21 years to write off your investment. I thought if I asked for 100 per cent they would whittle me down, so I'd better ask for more.

BK: 150?

JS: Yes, 150 per cent, with 50 per cent of investment returns tax free. As it turned out, it wasn't whittled down in the normal inter-departmental process, so it was a supercharged incentive – the industry certainly took off. We made it fraud-proof for foreigners, so that the people that deserved to be able to work with higher budgets and make international-scale films were Australians; they got the money to make their films. It is some satisfaction for me that it was the only tax incentive for films anywhere in the world that wasn't ripped off by the Hollywood studios.

It was a tremendous take-off point for the industry over the next three to four years. Great films were made; great talents came through – cinematographers, recording people, directors, producers – it was a tremendous time. So it was like a private equity exercise, or a venture capital exercise but on an industry scale.

BK: Innovation can take so many forms. So how do you go from that to building this business?

JS: After that I got married, had a child and took a year off to travel around Europe. It made me realise that Australia really is a new country where ideas drive things. Compared with Europe, Australia is a meritocracy; if you've got a good idea you can really do something with it.

'Compared with Europe, Australia is a meritocracy; if you've got a good idea you can really do something with it.'

When I came back, I did a venture capital investment. It was a high-tech coatings company that was developing a faster high tech, smarter way to apply clear coatings to timber products; a professor at the University of New South Wales started the idea. I worked on that for three years and then we sold it. It was a good practical operating level experience for me. That's when I had a yarn with

Bill, and in 1987 we decided to form an institutionally funded venture-capital firm, Australian Mezzanine Investments (AMIL). That was before the crash in October 1987. It was a challenge in those early days, raising the money, but the other part was pioneering a new industry sector in Australia. Again, there were so many institutional barriers; long-term capital was largely locked up.

'There were so many institutional barriers;
long-term capital was largely locked up.'

BK: Those structures are not that different now in terms of the conflicts around personal advice.

JS: Yes, but at that time, it was a superannuation manager old-boy network led by the AMP and National Mutual. They did a bundled service, so they would do the actuarial work, the pension entitlement work, the insurance work, the investment management work and the investor communications work – all of it. Despite all of that we managed to get a couple of investors who hadn't outsourced the whole of their superannuation investment to one of these majors, but were doing it internally. Brave souls, they were terrific: Phil Kelly at State Super, was first in,

followed by CSR, Shell, and BHP. They made decisions based on backing a good idea and looking at what we'd done individually. They realised we had scars on our back – we had learnt the ropes, made our mistakes and learnt from them – and decided to give us a go.

BK: So in 1987, Bill was 42 and you were 38 when you had these really formative experiences. It is interesting that many of these companies put their money entirely with someone else to handle. Was the reason you got some traction with the four early investors that they had some in-house management of some of their money?

JS: Yes, that's the only reason: they had in-house management and they had people who were prepared to take a risk. The traditional thing for a Superannuation Trustee was to have an external adviser, who would look at ten-year track records of potential managers like us, and if it stacked up, make the investment. By definition, in Australia private equity and venture capital didn't have a ten-year record; somebody had to create it. So I take my hat off to those brave people who made those decisions at: CSR, Shell, State Super and BHP. Indeed, I am so grateful to them, and all the other investors who gave us the opportunity to pioneer private equity in Australia, including the first investors from overseas who joined our program in 2000. It is amazing to look back at our original fund of $30 million in 1987 that seeded an industry now managing $30 billion!

BK: That's interesting, because this is before the crash. Over the last five and definitely ten years, getting some of the big houses to allocate a venture capital or to allocate a private equity is still incredibly difficult.

Then there is the recent Royal Commission into Misconduct in the Banking, Superannuation and Financial Services Industry; let alone them investing into private companies or anywhere that might be public infrastructure.

JS: Super funds are meant to be there for the benefit of their members.

BK: That's the theory.

JS: Retaining – not losing – members is a good corporate idea. I saw that Ian Silk from Australian Super was arguing that spending money on strategies to retain and grow your member numbers is in itself a good thing because you get economies of scale and the fee structure for members goes down. So far so good.

However, in terms of advertising for member acquisition/retention, you can't advertise your returns because you've got to say they're not a predicator for the future. What you can advertise is your cost structure, making the obvious point that if it's lower, then all things being equal, you'll have more money at the end of the day. Obviously, the industry funds trade heavily on that.

Cost is measured by the Management Expense Ratio (MER), but its structure is incredibly difficult for us in private equity. Typically, private equity has two components in its fee structure: an annual management fee, say 2 per cent; and a 20 per cent profit share after a hurdle rate of return. Hence the oft used term of "2 and 20". However, it's actually "2 or 20", because to collect the 20 per cent you have to clear a hurdle rate of net returns, net of all fees and expenses charged previously.

BK: So where's the management fee?

JS: But for MER purposes, it's an annual calculation. You show your 2 per cent every year, and then in the year you take a profit share you show the 20 per cent, but you can't go back and show that the 2 per cent recorded annually up to then has been rebated. So the MER double counts the cost of PE.

The more successful the private equity investment you've made, the higher that 20 per cent share is in terms of dollars – the higher your management expense ratio, and the worse it looks for the superfunds advertising: a perverse outcome!

No American investor has ever asked us our MER costs; they've always asked us for our net return after costs. Whereas Australian investors say, can't you lower your fees? So what's best for members? The advertising posture to retain and grow members or the net returns to members?

BK: Cash, or cash returns?

JS: Compared to their peers around the world, Australian superfunds are way underweight private asset classes like PE, and member returns are lower as a result.

BK: People talk more about strategy in business than structure. I have formed the view that structure is at least as important and potentially much more important. I always think of it as a cyclist on a bike: the rigidity of the bike is the structure, and the structure is what delivers the power to perform.

JS: It's a structural conversation as to why they're not investing enough in this asset class.

BK: And structural reform, or structure discussion, is very hard.

JS: I'm not crying poor because we've raised all the money we needed offshore. When we formed AMIL we realised that we're up against this embedded institutional stranglehold on long term capital.

BK: ... the structure of the system.

JS: Yes. So we formed an industry association; I was a foundation director.

BK: The Australian Private Equity and Venture Capital Association Limited (AVCAL)?

JS: Yes, we formed AVCAL in the late 1980s. I convened the first national conference; we dug deep and brought in some overseas speakers. We needed to legitimise the class here because the incumbent superannuation managers like the AMP started putting it about that private equity wasn't a suitable class for superannuation. It was too high risk and wouldn't pass the "Prudent Man" test that every trustee has to ask themselves: is this a suitable risk–reward ratio for a widow and an orphan?

The answer was very easy. You have in a portfolio cash at one end, which is super secure and makes you lower returns, and then you have high risk at the other end with high return. It's about the balance. You don't take any asset in isolation; you look at the balance of the portfolio.

The answer may have been easy, but it didn't suit the insurance companies that didn't have a product to offer in that area, and they found reasons to knock off the product. We needed an industry association to lobby and argue the asset class, to get it accepted as it was internationally. The real breakthrough came with the industry superfunds. I remember going to the first conference of the industry superfunds in Wollongong. The big insurers were there, patronising the workers.

It was really interesting because they were saying they could help; they could do all of it and they were shocked to see the Industry Fund movement pull the whole model of handled superannuation apart and invite separately bids to manage the component of insurance, funds management by asset class, communication etc. This was terrific for members as it lowered the overall costs, and it allowed private equity to bid in as an asset class on its own merits.

BK: Who did that?

JS: This innovation was led by Bill Kelty and Garry Weaven, lowering costs and opening up to more asset classes has borne fruit – the industry funds have early outperformed the traditional incumbent commercial managers.

BK: What else had to change for PE to succeed?

JS: Three things. Debt: Accessing debt was the next challenge – banks were not used to lending against budgeted cash flows rather than bricks and mortar and other tangible securities. Slowly they came into this sector with modest lending ratios. Today they have plenty of competition from non-bank lenders.

Deal Flow: Back then if an investment banker suggested to a client wanting to sell a business that apart from trade sale or IPO you could invite management to buy out the business you would be shown the door – today you would lose your job if you didn't include PE as an exit option.

People: But the biggest change I've seen is in people. In those days, we were asking executives to take a salary cut and mortgage their house to put money into a business. It was high risk and it had not been done before, was it sensible?

'The biggest change I've seen is in people.'

Today, there are so many examples of success. Just in our AMIL/CHAMP portfolio story so far, there would be well over 350 Executives of companies that we've invested in that have made more than a million dollars each through management equity schemes. That has meant more executives are actively looking to be involved in Private Equity today making it a talent advantage for private equity. Many high-flying executives are absolutely exhausted by the risk-averse atmosphere in listed public companies. The idea is that if you grow your earnings per share by 3-4 per cent per annum, keep your dividends steady, have a high pay-out ratio, then why would you take a risk?

And if you've got a new idea, you've got to float it up in a very high level of principle. If it doesn't get shot down in flames at the first board meeting, you're asked to flesh it out for the second board meeting. Then you get asked lots of questions, and if you're lucky, by the third or fourth board meeting, you might get a cautious go decision.

That's very frustrating for people who really want to build things. So our ability to attract the best and brightest whenever there's a hole in the management team that we're backing is a key thing that has changed radically since we started AMIL 30 years ago.

You can attract the best talent you need and you're up against very slow-moving, publicly listed, conservatively managed competitors in the marketplace. In my opinion, these are very good settings for private equity, but while for the sake of Australia I'd like the major public company boardrooms to be far more growth orientated, for the sake of private equity, I am happy to have it stay as it is, so I'm conflicted on my values.

'So while for the sake of Australia I'd like the major public company boardrooms to be far more growth-orientated, for the sake of private equity, I am happy to have it stay as it is!'

BK: Definitely. Big lessons. So what has helped you achieve your goals?

JS: If I think back, and this is not just in business, but one of the things that Bill and I did right from the start is we gave ourselves time out to do non-business things. Bill's done a couple of government inquiries, most recently his chairmanship of Innovation and Science Australia. He was previously chairman of Austrade. I've chaired the Sydney Opera House, SBS, the Australian Film School, the National Capital Planning Authority – I've been on about 20 not-for-profit boards so far.

Whether it's in business or the not-for-profit sector, I'd say the same thing – it's about having the right people, the right idea, and the right timing. Those three things have to flow together. It's not to do with making money; it's to do with achieving an objective. The objective in the not-for-profit area is not money, it's an outcome, which is measured in social benefits. You have to be clear about the idea, the problem that's being solved, how that's going to be solved, and how you know if you're solving it. That applies to business as well.

Interestingly, people often think it's a very different thing running private equity to running a government operation like the Sydney Opera House. It's not, because most of the not-for-profit sector is underfunded. You've got to be really good at managing resources because the size of the problem is always bigger than the funding available.

BK: Which is where private equity gets involved.

JS: Similarly when you're backing entrepreneurs, their idea is always bigger than the money they've got. So again, it's about being very clear on what you're trying to do, the best way of achieving it, and being very frugal in the way you use your resources. The fashionable phrase now is failing fast, meaning you need to recognise early if your current strategy is not working, work out why, pivot to a new direction. I'm amazed at how often people hit a brick wall and then complain about who built the wall rather than work out how to get around it.

'I'm amazed at how often people hit a brick wall and then complain about who built the wall rather than work out how to get around it.'

BK: Failing fast. What about succeeding fast?

JS: It's all about timing. Is the problem really hot now and have you got a solution that's wonderful and elegant? We have had varied experience. For example, Fingerscan – biometric recognition – it was about 10 years ahead of its time in terms of mass deployment, and today it's everywhere. LookSmart was a great idea, and the time was right. Austal – fast catamaran ferries – was another one of our early successes; it was terrific too. But let me emphasise that success often comes from doing ordinary things better; it doesn't have to be a totally new idea.

'Very often, success comes from doing ordinary things better; it doesn't have to be a totally new idea.'

So coming back to the people, as I mentioned, honesty and integrity is the first test. If you don't pass that, you're out. Then it's about knowing how to execute an idea and how to bring people along with you; it requires creative thinking and a huge drive. Entrepreneurs need to live, eat and sleep the mission. They need to bring people along with them, but not be so driven that they don't listen to anyone else, they need to be open to be challenged about exactly how they

are implementing their plans. That combination makes the best leaders. You can apply those skills to a very ordinary business. You just have to do it a hell of a lot better than anybody else. Conversely, a great idea in bad hands is a sure way to lose money. But an ordinary idea in good hands; you might not make a fortune, but you'll do okay. It's the combination.

'Entrepreneurs need to live, eat and sleep the mission. They need to bring people along with them, but not be so driven that they don't listen to anyone else.'

Another key factor is clarity of purpose. A great example is Austar, one of our most successful investments. They got caught up in the dotcom era in a whole frenzy of triple plays. It was pay television, it was internet, it was telephony, and it was all going to be bundled together. They got up to a valuation of $7 billion on the Australian stock market while blowing red ink on their profit and loss statement.

The lenders had supplied $700 million, and they were doing an earnings before interest, tax, depreciation and amortisation (EBITDA) of minus $40 million, on a debt of $700 million – frankly, it was a very dangerous situation they were in. The stock market pulled back and they came down from $7 billion to $117 million in market cap – it was pretty dramatic. We thought the market had oversold. Whilst its true to say the stock market usually gets it right in the long run, at any given moment it can be over or under valued.

'Whilst it's true to say that the stock market usually gets it right in the long run, at any given moment it can be over or under valued.'

We decided to have a go and turned that company around with exactly the same management team, so it's not all about changing managers, sometimes it's just clarity of focus and rigour in execution. In this case, they were distracted and trying to do too many things at once. We took BSkyB as our model of what a well-run pay television business looked like and took advantage of Austar's pay television monopoly. Monopolies are wonderful things. Capitalism is supposed to excel by competition I have yet to meet a capitalist who didn't hanker after a monopoly.

'Monopolies are wonderful things. Capitalism is supposed to excel by competition but I have yet to meet a capitalist who didn't hanker after a monopoly.'

Our business plan didn't call for anything heroic – there were just minor increases in revenue – but a complete change in the cost structure meant Austar was making $100 million profit on the bottom line in a couple of years and we sold at a great profit.

BK: Was it a trade sale? Public to private and then trade sale?

JS: We never privatised it; it remained public but we were able to move to control through a creative process, the international theory of comity. Normally you can't buy more than 19.9 per cent without making a public offer, and at that point, you have drawn attention to the opportunity, and have set up an "auction" environment against yourself. So how to avoid that? We talked to a number of law firms, before we came to one lawyer who said, 'Look, I know the answer before you even finish talking, but I don't know how to charge you because an hourly rate isn't going to do it, is it?' We agreed on a million-dollar success fee.

BK: Can you expand on that?

JS: It was about the Chapter 11 process on the hold co debt in America being called a public markets transaction; regulators in the two countries should cooperate in order not to frustrate the operations. So if we did it over there first, and we got the hold co debt, converted it into op co equity, so we walked in to 50 per cent of the equity of Austar operating by the conversion of the hold co debt before the market became aware.

We bought the hold co debt at a discount and converted it into share ownership. We then then offered the public a similar equivalent value for their shares but by this time they knew we were on to something so nobody wanted to sell out; they just sat there. So we had 50 per cent, and another strategic shareholder had 25 per cent. Between us we had 75 per cent and we could run the company the way we wanted to, but it stayed public. When it came time to exit we did one of those overnight sell downs.

BK: Block traded it?

JS: Yes, it was one of the early block trades that was pioneered by Simon Mordant

in his previous shop Caliburn. It was a great result for our investors in CHAMP, and also for the public investors who stayed in for the ride. So there was a very creative way to get into control, and a creative exit, but critically on the way through a new targeted operational focus very well executed by the CEO.

BK: You've briefly mentioned not changing people faster – what was your biggest mistake?

JS: Sometimes people get themselves in to the wrong position or get overpromoted. We try hard to work with people already in the companies we acquire. You hope they'll change and grow into the job. When you look back, it's a generic mistake not recognising that it isn't going to work. For everybody's sake, make a change. That's probably the biggest area of regret that most of us in this industry have, not just us.

BK: Last question. What's the one thing that's made your 30-year partnership with Bill Ferris work?

JS: That's an easy one: we think differently and we respect those differences, we have complimentary skills. It's clear that together the two of us end up with a far better analysis than either of us could on our own.

'Together the two of us end up with a far better analysis than either of us could on our own.'

It's also personality; Bill's a very tolerant chap, he puts up with me. It's been a gift in life for me to have a wonderful life partner in Ros, my wife, and a wonderful business partner in Bill. I would say that in 30 years I've spent more time with Bill than I have with my wife – and I've had fewer arguments with him than with my wife, but they have both been wonderful partnerships.

It's not often that you can look back on a 30-year business partnership and say that in all honesty, while there's been robust discussion, we've never really had a real fight – it's a blessing to be able to look back on a business partnership and be able to say that.

BK: That's great: most people never get to meet someone who really changes their life. Thank you.

INVESTMENT WISDOM LESSONS

• Do good
It's about values in everything you do.

• See clearly
Clarity about what to value in life.

• Trust is number one
Strasser's number one rule was: never invest with people you don't trust.

Alex Waislitz

Chairman, Thorney Investments

'Whilst I still am aspirational and want to do well, it's great to be able to have an impact on other people's lives.'

Alex Waislitz is Executive Chairman and Founder of the Thorney Investment Group, a privately-owned, Melbourne-based, diversified investor in public securities, private companies and property. He is also Vice President of the Collingwood Football Club.

Thorney specialises in investing in emerging companies across a broad array of industries including Manufacturing, Technology, Mining Services and Resources. Media reports have estimated the value of Thorney's investment portfolio at well in excess of $1 billion.

Alex is also Chairman of Thorney Opportunities Limited and Thorney Technologies Limited, ASX-listed investment companies which he formed to allow individual shareholders to invest alongside the private Thorney Investment Group.

He also has a strong interest in philanthropy. In 2014 he established the Waislitz Foundation with the aim of donating $50 million to charity. The Foundation has supported the eradication of global poverty, indigenous education, heart surgery for children in developing countries and homelessness.

Alex is a graduate of Monash University in Law and Commerce and a Graduate of the Harvard Business School OPM Program.

www.thorneyopportunities.com.au

Interview

BRETT KELLY: How did you get started in investing?

ALEX WAISLITZ: I was interested in the buy side, not the sell side. I wanted to be where the deals were initiated or transacted upon, as I was suited more to the front end of that. I wasn't particularly good at the selling side. I didn't see myself as a salesman type or a marketing type. I thought of myself more as analysing, assessing and questioning how business could be run. And I was stimulated by how to improve businesses.

'I thought of myself more as analysing, assessing and questioning how business could be run. And I was interested, stimulated by how to improve businesses.'

BK: What scope was there in that role to do that? Were you just analysing and going?

AW: There wasn't a huge scope to do that. It was more driven, I suppose, ultimately by sales and that's why I left, even though I had a great time and it was a great introduction to New York. At that point, I realised that I wanted to stay longer in New York than a year or so. In doing so, I realised that I wanted to get more onto that buy side of the equation. I ultimately ended up working for Robert Holmes à Court, and was part of the opening of his New York operations through Bell Group. This was in the mid-1980s.

BK: So, you're still very young, 26 or 27.

AW: Yes, I'm about 25, 26, thereabouts.

BK: And that's 1985, thereabouts.

AW: Yes, thereabouts, 1985, yes. I worked with him in a terrifically exciting environment, because he didn't have a lot of US assets at the time. In fact, some investments, but from an operating point of view, he had some entertainment distribution and production company which came out of the acquisition he made in the UK of Lord Lew Grade's operation called ITC. But within 18 months we had built up an excess of $1 billion of investments, particularly across the resources area.

BK: And were you doing the analysis business case? How did Robert Holmes à Court do a deal?

AW: There was only two of us who opened the office at the time. Another lawyer who was more focused purely on the law and legal issues. And by default, I became the...

BK: Deal guy.

AW: The treasury guy, the dealer in terms of the market and the options, equities, and whatever else came up that was of commercial interest to the group. I was part of what they called the treasury, an investment group, which was a global group out of Melbourne, Perth, London, and then this fledgling New York operation.

It was a group of smart, energetic, motivated people, led directly by Holmes à Court ultimately at the top of the tree. And I was lucky enough, even though I was young, to get a bit of his personal attention, because I was the guy in New York. And he was often in New York, but he was often on the phone from all different parts of the globe, because he didn't sleep too much.

It was a great honour to work for him, and I learned a tremendous amount in a relatively short period of time. So, I was there for about roughly four years. And that was right through the 1987 crash, which was all hype and growth up until the crash.

We saw the other side of the mountain, where it was all about trying to survive and liquefy some of the assets, and do my little bit to help to stay intact.

'We saw the other side of the mountain, where it was all about trying to survive and liquefy some of the assets, and do my little bit to help to stay intact.'

BK: If there were one or two things that you think that you learned from Robert Holmes à Court, what do you think they would be?

AW: I think on the positive side, I would say be contrarian, be brave, do thorough analysis, be intuitive, and leave yourself alternative paths.

BK: Did you think that he was a great analyst, or a great lawyer, or a great strategic person? Obviously, these guys are good at all of those things.

AW: I thought he was a brilliant thinker, and he was a terrific negotiator.

BK: What makes a terrific negotiator?

AW: I think knowing how far to push a situation, having the courage of your conviction. I think good negotiators can put themselves in the other stakeholders' position and conclude what would be regarded as a win for them, and work out how far you could push.

BK: To still deliver a win.

AW: And he pushed to the maximum in doing so, and got outcomes that probably many others would not have got.

BK: How does a guy who is that bright and that successful have the 1987 crash happen to him in the way that it does?

AW: Some of the negatives that we have learnt was that I think even though he saw value in a lot of things and he was right, I believe he pursued too many opportunities at the same time. He was too widespread and too exposed.

BK: Too broad.

AW: Too many battles in too many geographies and too many jurisdictions. It had stretched the bandwidth of the financial resources, and the management team probably too far. At the same time as that, using too much financial leverage. Whether that would be from borrowings or exposures for example, huge exposures on BHB, open put options, for example, which ended up costing a fortune to unwind.

BK: Why was that? Obviously, information's much more broadly available now. I can go on YouTube and watch thousands of hours of Warren Buffet teaching you whatever you want to learn. That wasn't available easily then. But how do you end up there?

AW: It could be a combination of the success he'd had up to there. If you don't keep your feet on the ground, so to speak, and you believe that it can go on forever. The markets were euphoric, and it seemed like there was plenty of funding around that was being led aggressively to entrepreneurial corporate titans.

I think one of the lessons there is even though funds are available, it doesn't mean you should always take them. Because if you take them, you're inclined to use them and invest it, and I think that's a little bit what happened. So, you get on a merry go round, and then you get challenged. We have that situation in the market now. In theory, you would say you should be borrowing as much as you can now, because interest rates are low. But what happens also when interest rates are low is that you get asset bubbles, because people are chasing yield for example, and in chasing yield they often don't understand the risks that they're taking on. At some point, there's usually a day of reckoning.

'The markets were euphoric... there was plenty of funding around... I think one of the lessons is even though funds are available, it doesn't mean you should always take them.'

BK: So, you're on Wall Street, there's going to be a crash, but no one knows. Could you feel it? Did you see it? Did anyone? A lot of people saw it after the event, they'd tell you.

AW: I wouldn't say that, I was pretty naïve. I was still young in the game. I had not experienced a crash before, other than hearing about it as some event that happened many years ago. So, I certainly didn't anticipate it in any meaningful way. Whenever I would question anyone about some of these exposures, or how we're doing too much there, I wouldn't get much response because I was the junior member for the team.

BK: So, you have to give the news to Robert Holmes à Court that the market's crashed?

AW: Yes.

BK: It happened in the afternoon, didn't it? Near closing.

AW: It was the Friday, the market had already gone down. And then, Monday, which later became known as Black Monday, I think followed suit with even more aggression. I actually called my immediate boss who was in London, Allen Newman. He said to me, you call Robert and give him the news, because you're in New York and you're live there in front of the screen.

BK: And where was Robert at that time?

AW: Robert was in Perth.

BK: So, tell me how did that go down?

AW: I called him in Perth and I don't know what hour it was, but it was certainly not daylight hours. And I think his wife answered the phone, Janet, and she put Robert on the phone, and I just told him. In my unsure voice, because I couldn't understand really what was happening.

Every minute, really, as you looked at the screen, it was going down further. I'd never seen anything like this, so I didn't know really what to make of it. I just told him that the market was plunging. He was actually pretty calm. I think I may have woken him. He said, it's the indexes, whatever it was.

I said the particular stocks that we were involved in are getting hammered. He took the information in. He was silent. He was very good at silence. When you go back to negotiating, he was a master of using silence as a tool of negotiation because he had this intimidating manner, and when he was silent, somehow other people cracked and just kept talking at the other end. And he got the information. But really, he didn't say anything other than call me back in 15 minutes. I suspect he was getting up and checking it himself, or whatever.

I called him back in 15, 20 minutes. I gave him a further update. It was further down. And that's when he seemed to have then called all the troops, and everyone was starting to call in. Everyone was like, what do we do? So, I was awaiting my instructions at that point.

BK: When you called back, that 15 minutes later, he was all over what was happening?

AW: He wasn't all over it, but you could see that he'd checked the information, and he was starting to think about it. Then I got a call to start selling a few things.

BK: And off you went.

AW: And off I went.

BK: What's the enduring lesson for you from what you saw in that period? And how do you think that relates to where we are now?

AW: Yes, as I said a key thing for me is not to stretch yourself too thin in terms of management bandwidth. And that's constantly a challenge that I try to impose here. And it is a challenge, because every investment manager you have wants to be active and seize ideas. I guess I've got to look at it from the helicopter perspective and say, where are our exposures and how many?

My rule of thumb basically is that an active experienced manager can probably only handle 10 to 20 investment positions with depth of knowledge and being up to date.

'My rule of thumb basically is that an active experienced manager can probably handle 10-20 investment positions with depth of knowledge and being up to date.'

Maybe another same amount again with a good working knowledge that they're on the watch list. So, I try to keep within the bandwidth. That's my job, to constantly try to cull or probe, or do that. Other lessons are unless you've got a cash flow business that you've got alongside you, be very cognisant, sensible, more conservative than aggressive on the amount of debt that you borrow.

So, for example, with Thorney, although we have a much wider portfolio, but over the journey we've focused a lot on microcaps stocks, small cap stocks, midcap stocks. Both public and private. Particularly, obviously in private. There's virtually no liquidity, and even in the listed in those areas, there's limited liquidity. So, don't pretend there's liquidity when there isn't liquidity. When you do need liquidity, it gaps. The share price can gap down, and you still may not have enough buyers. So, I've taken a very conservative approach. Some would argue and say, against those exposures we've got very little or no debt.

BK: What do you say is little?

AW: Little is zero.

BK: Less than 20 per cent?

AW: Yes. And often zero. In fact, we usually run with a surplus of cash to take advantage of when inevitable market corrections happen.

My view is that you should, if you are successfully managed, be able to get a good enough return. We've been able to demonstrate that over 20 odd years, that you don't need to use the leverage to achieve that return on those types of exposures. If we're dealing with larger cap stocks or other things, property assets with income, we might have some debt sensibly against them.

But my father I think was fearful of debt from the old European style, and the paranoia of not owing anybody. It probably limited his growth in his property development. But again, ultimately he was successful.

BK: He survived.

AW: But at a slower pace. My view was, I can withstand the volatility of the market if I'm not overexposed to debt. That's pretty much what I've done with Thorney.

*'My view was, I can withstand the volatility of the market
if I'm not overexposed to debt.'*

BK: So, when did you start Thorney out of New York?

AW: I started it part-time in Australia, in the latter part of 1991.

BK: And how is the business structured? Is it owned by the managers?

AW: No, it's always been a small group. A niche player, I suppose. I never really wanted to be a big manager of people, and have a big army of people. I was more about getting good returns, and growing off a tight base, rather than having scale for scale's sake.

*'I was more about getting good returns, and growing off a tight
base, rather than having scale for scale's sake.'*

We run a very flat structure. We pretty much have an open-door policy, and people can come in and talk about whatever at any time of the day. No one is really pigeonholed, everyone gets an opportunity to grow and develop. But what we have is some senior investment analysts who have responsibilities, to suggest, recommend, follow positions. They have a certain amount of authority, and anything beyond that is usually run by me as the chief investment officer. We have junior analysts who will support those senior ones, and so on. We have finance and administration beyond that.

BK: And how many people?

AW: We have under 20 people, including a couple of people overseas.

BK: Where are they? In New York?

AW: One person in Los Angeles, one in New York. Other than that, the rest are here in Australia. We have some people who manage the real estate side.

BK: And the capital that you manage is your own and wholesale investors'?

AW: No, the principal investment company, the one we started is a private company. No outside investors. That was the journey for about 20 years, up to about five or so years ago, when we took over a failed public company and transitioned it into a listed investment company called Thorney Opportunities. Even though I'm the largest shareholder, that does have other shareholders.

BK: Did the private company roll into that?

AW: The private company, that's a new vehicle. The private company invested in that company. Roughly 30 per cent. And then 70 per cent is owned by public shareholders.

BK: And what was the raise initially?

AW: 50.

BK: 50, and you guys put in 15?

AW: And we put in 15, yes.

BK: And what did you see as the benefit of that?

AW: What we found as we got bigger, we were looking at more companies with the same attitude of being constructivist. We wanted to really do a couple of things, have a vehicle where we could use the profile of a public company to better help in engagement with the other companies we were looking to invest in. We had an obligation to report to our shareholders on these companies, on our view on these companies. I just felt that it would assist us in better engagement with the company. If they didn't engage, we would be able to highlight that through the media or through our letters to shareholders about what we thought should be happening, and what's not happening.

BK: So, do you call yourself constructivist because you don't like activist?

AW: Yes.

BK: Because no-one likes an activist in Australia.

AW: I don't have a problem with activism conceptually, as opposed to being a passive investor. That is our style. But active to me doesn't always imply hostility. Active to me implies engagement, communicating, and debate.

'Active implies engagement, communication, and debate.'

BK: But why don't we have hostile, "horrible" activists in Australia?

AW: I would say 70 per cent, 80 per cent, 90 per cent of our times dealing with management, we've had a good response. But occasionally, we've had an outbreak of disagreement. It's resulted in us contacting other shareholders to see if they have got the same view as us or not. If they do, then we put more pressure on the company to affect the changes we're talking about. We've been quite successful, I think, in that regard.

Again, pointing out to those who are charged with the responsibility of managing, that they are doing it on behalf of the owners, who are the shareholders. We are not just one stakeholder, we are a key stakeholder. But just to round that out, a few years later we did the same thing with the second public vehicle, which was failing. In that case, we took control of it actually through an administrator.

We repurposed it as a second listed investment company focused on the technology investing space, Thorney Technologies. And the reason for that one was to offer shareholders a unique opportunity with what we thought was a unique idea, which was to create a company that could invest in technology at all levels. That is to say, not only in public...

BK: In the lifecycle.

AW: In the lifecycle, yes, it's what I've said. So, not only in public technology companies, but pre-IPO and even earlier stage. And also, global. Ultimately we've got both those vehicles in our style of boutique sizes. I'm the largest shareholder in both of them, but they have a different focus. The technology one, obviously on technology. Thorney Opportunities more value-based, and where we can see the opportunity to be a part of a catalyst for change.

BK: So, the benefit of that as opposed to it being a private firm? The disengagement of profile perhaps?

AW: I think there's a couple of things. It is permanent capital. It lifted our profile and enabled us to engage with a lot of the management. It enabled us to position ourselves better, for example, in the tech and the pre-IPO opportunities, because they wanted our name on board, and they wanted the ongoing engagement with our shareholders to be more visible, rather than more of a black box private company. It was a new challenge. It was also you have to stimulate yourself to keep growing, you have to stimulate the people who work within Thorney for new challenges.

That was part of it as well. We've been successful, fortunately, on both of those two, which could lead to other vehicles in the future. Be it here or for overseas investment.

BK: How old are you now?

AW: I'm 61, and still engaged and active, and still enjoying it. My father worked until he passed at 87, and he was working up until three months before he passed. Doing other hobbies and things that he liked, but still engaged in work. And I actually noticed that a lot of his friends and colleagues who retired earlier in their 60s...

BK: Died earlier.

AW: Died earlier.

BK: Yes, I think that's true. Just to finish off, a couple of questions. The most important investment lesson, if you had to choose one?

AW: Buy. Buy well.

BK: And system versus gap feel?

AW: I once went up to Lindsay Fox and talked to him. I said to Lindsay, who I liked, 'Lindsay, you must get lots of deal opportunities every day, and how do you process that?' He told me, 'I've got all these analysts who do the numbers and they give me all these spreadsheets. Mate, I left school at 13, I pat my tummy and when my gut feels good, those are the ones I do.'

I may be more professionally trained with a legal background and commerce and in accounting, so I do like to have the background analysis and all the data. We still make sure we diligently do that. But we also look at very subjective, probably, elements, which is our view on the management or the leadership of the company.

Particularly in those small and mid-sized companies, they're so critical. They're critical anyway in any organisation, but in particular because they don't have the breadth or the bigger balance sheet to withstand mistakes.

So, if you don't believe in the people, then that is a big negative for us in terms of deciding. Or, if we believe dramatically in the business, but we don't like the people, then we need to be active quickly to make those changes.

BK: To try and change it.

AW: We'll back the people that we believe are good. Our judgement over the years has been pretty high in terms of success rate there. Where we like particularly a business, or the underlying opportunity there, and we don't believe in the people, then we will make an assessment whether we can be successful in creating a changed environment.

If we can, then we'll try to get on with it and improve the board, or the chairman, or indeed the CEO or CFO. That's been a big part of our investing style. So, the answer to it is intuition backed with financial analysis.

'So, the answer is intuition backed with financial analysis.'

BK: If you could give yourself one piece of advice as a younger man at 18 or earlier, what would that be?

AW: Believe in yourself and have a go.

BK: Final question, there were two things I noticed when I came to your office. One was the very substantial giving history of the group in terms of Operation Heart and different things, and the other one is you can't miss the parties outside. There's a great Carrie Parker quote that losers have meetings and winners have parties. What's the theory on the giving and the parties?

AW: I worked for Richard Pratt for a long time, and he used to have an expression of 'Celebrate the successes, share the successes with the people who helped you be successful'. In his case, it was include the customers, and in our case our customer equivalent might be brokers or bankers, and indeed, the management of the companies that we invest in. So, you have to enjoy the journey. I've always believed in that. I believe in celebrating the success. Build a foundation of people that you enjoy working with, and you enjoy going on that journey with.

'Build a foundation of people that you enjoy working with, and you enjoy going on that journey with.'

I've got lots of interests in my life, and I don't believe in segmenting them fully. I believe you should cross-pollinate with different people, different cultures, different interests. I think you learn from all the experiences, and so I believe you should celebrate all those experiences with all those people at the same time. Then, suddenly you've got a group of people and suddenly it's a party size. But it was also with thought. When I started Thorney I had a problem, because I didn't have any capital and I didn't have enough contacts or networks in the brokerage community for example, in the investment community. So, I thought to myself, how can I make an impact?

'Suddenly, from not having a network of people, we got brokers who were interested in talking to me and were putting forward ideas.'

BK: What year was this roughly?

AW: This was in '92, when I started Thorney on a full-time basis.

BK: And you wanted to have the best party.

AW: No, it was more than just the party. The party was partly networking and meeting people. Secondly, we introduced at each of our parties and still do, the concept of a prize. The prize was to reward someone who had made a great contribution to Thorney, by way of an idea that we acted on and were successful on, or indeed helped us avoid a big mistake, or something along those lines. But usually something that we were successful, had a successful outcome in.

And even though I didn't have a lot of funds, I made the decision to take a risk and give a meaningful prize. So, an overseas trip, a boat. The first one was a Ferrari car. I was giving away things that I didn't have myself, actually. But I thought it was something that made an impact.

'Even though I didn't have a lot of funds, I made the decision to take a risk and give a meaningful prize. The first one was a Ferrari car... I was giving away things that I didn't have myself.'

BK: That's so smart.

AW: It would be a feature that no one else was doing. And that proved to be great. Some of the other things that we did at the time were, as I said we had very little money, how are we going to get stockbrokers with a new idea to come and talk to us? So, I had to give the impression that we were transaction focused, that we would act. But what I did tangibly is, I actually went to many of them and said, 'I'll pay you double the commission that you normally get, but in doing so, I want you to call me first.'

BK: Smart.

AW: And suddenly, from not having a network of people, we got brokers who were interested in talking to me and were putting forward ideas.

BK: So, institutional brokers?

AW: Institutional, retail. It was more retail I suppose. It was still at the retail level, but the good retail brokers. Some were overlapped with institutional. So, in addition to searching for our own idea, which is primarily what we found, we got a good cadre of brokers coming in with good ideas. And then, our challenge was to cull those ideas and cull those brokers as to who we thought were reliable and worthy, to the point where if they said have a look at something, we would say, they're a good quality advisor. And, the parties got their own momentum too...

'The parties got their own momentum, too...'

BK: How many people were there?

AW: The last party we had was 500, or 600. Maybe more. It was 700, I think. It was very important that the partners were invited, and I wanted those people who were invited, their partners to say to them, 'Keep working with Thorney because we want to be at the next party!' And we made sure the parties were good. There was entertainment, camaraderie, music, good food. Overseas trips were another thing that I did. When I had started doing well I thought, how can I engage also with these good advisors or new advisors when we're still not very big in the scheme of things?

BK: And you would take them over?

AW: I would take them overseas. I would say, let's have an experience together, and let's go to places, that many hadn't been to at the time, to Shanghai, or Beijing, Mongolia. We went to Europe, America, Russia, and all these places. The whole idea was to enjoy life, educate yourself with smart people. And everywhere we went, we included business meetings. So, we did lots of fun things as well, but we made sure it had a business focus.

BK: How long were the trips, one week?

AW: Usually it was a week, 10 days, something like that.

BK: And just the broker, not their partners?

AW: Just the brokers on that one. Again, we had some great journeys, including with people you mentioned before, David Paradice and Jeff Wilson were two who have been on many trips with me. And that also became a feature of what we did, that others didn't do. And the institutional brokerage firms couldn't do, because they had restrictions. As a private company, I could do that. And again, I learnt a lot from Richard Pratt as to how he entertained his customers and went about it.

BK: Schooling.

AW: Yes, schooling for me.

BK: Fantastic. I want to thank you so much for your time today. It's been absolutely excellent.

AW: In terms of the foundation, just to finish off on the giving.

BK: Yes, on the giving.

AW: The giving also, I think I learnt that from my parents, from my mum. Even though they didn't have much, they always opened their home to people, to come in, other immigrants who they were slightly better off than, because they'd been a bit longer. So, we often had people, so to speak, straight off the ship.

BK: Off the boat.

AW: Off the boat, coming in. And hearing from an early age the heartache that they went through. My view was if you're fortunate enough to be able to give, try to share it. I learnt that also from my former wife, Heloise, and her generous nature, and her family. The Pratt Foundation is one of the biggest, and largest, and longest foundations in Australia. I always had a desire to, and did, work in the foundation. I always had the desire to be able to do my own community work.

'If you're fortunate enough to be able to give, try to share it.'

There are many wealthy people I know who give very little. There are others who are less wealthy who give a lot. So, it's interesting to see. Everyone's got a different approach. But I think I got the culture of giving from my parents. My parents were helped when they arrived, with an organisation called Jewish Care, which helped them get their first accommodation, and food stamps in the initial period, and helped my dad find his initial job. I guess those are just things you hear about at the kitchen table, that come through.

BK: Osmosis.

AW: Yes, an osmosis. Then, it was from having worked in the foundation and seeing the impact, travelling the globe. I like to go to out of the way places. I've been to many parts of Asia and Africa, where you see magnificent natural sights, and you see some horrendous living conditions. You realise that if you have some success in business – which we've had – and whilst I still am aspirational and want to do well, it's great to be able to have an impact on other people's lives as well, to a small degree.

I'm actually hoping over time, that within the next few years I'm spending 50 per cent of my time on the Waislitz Foundation, pursuing some of the initiatives that we've started, and new ones, hopefully. I've said publicly that I want to give away $50 million, at least, over this decade and we've already started that journey in the last few years

---

'I've said publicly that I want to give away $50 million, at least, over this decade and we've already started that journey in the last few years.'

I've actually funded quite a few millions of dollars in the Waislitz Foundation at the moment, which not only causes an obligation, because you have to pay 5 per cent of the foundation each year, it's great because it keeps us focused on what we can do next.

BK: It gives you a bit of a plan.

AW: It's also something that I'm trying to bring my children along with me. I want to do it whilst I can still go and enjoy and meet the people, these great people who are doing this work in different parts of the world.

BK: Thank you so much for your time today.

INVESTMENT WISDOM LESSONS

• Be contrarian

Be brave, do thorough analysis, be intuitive, and leave yourself alternative paths.

• Be realistic

Key thing for me is not to stretch yourself too thin in terms of management bandwidth.

• Buy

Buy well.

Notes

RELEASES

GREAT
AS GIFTS
ORDER YOUR
COPIES NOW

HARDBACK + SOFT COVER / 296 PAGES

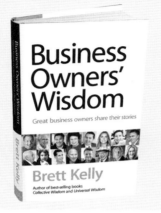

HARDBACK + SOFT COVER / 230 PAGES

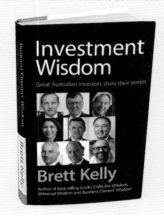

PRAISE FOR THE AUTHOR

"I liked his imagination and chutzpah, it was something quite different ...
I think he (Brett) is very much to be congratulated."

THE LATE HON. RJL HAWKE

"(Brett) showed great imagination ... persistence and thoughtfulness."

THE RT. HON. MALCOLM FRASER

"An inspiration ..."

MIRANDA DEVINE,
THE DAILY TELEGRAPH

"A very determined young bloke."

RAY MARTIN,
A CURRENT AFFAIR

HARDBACK / 326 PAGES

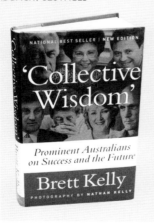

HARDBACK / 272 PAGES

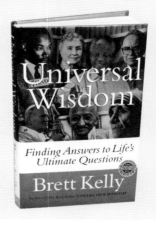

ORDER FORM

TO ORDER COPIES OF *COLLECTIVE WISDOM, UNIVERSAL WISDOM, BUSINESS OWNERS' WISDOM, INVESTMENT WISDOM* **FILL IN THE DETAILS AND SEND YOUR ORDER BY FAX, POST, EMAIL OR ONLINE** **www.brettkelly.com.au**

PLEASE PRINT CLEARLY

Full Name:

Delivery Address:

State: Postcode:

Tel: (   )   Mobile:

Fax: (   )

Email:

PAYMENT METHOD

Tick one of the following:

☐ Personal Cheque ☐ Bank Cheque ☐ Bankcard ☐ Visa ☐ Mastercard

Cheques payable to: 'Clown Publishing'

Cardholder's Name (as on card):

Card Number:

Expiry Date:

Cardholder's Signature:

QUANTITY OF BOOKS

☐	*INVESTMENT WISDOM* (Hardback) at **$49.95** each	$_____
☐	*INVESTMENT WISDOM* (Soft Cover) at **$39.95** each	$_____
☐	*COLLECTIVE WISDOM* (Hardback) at **$49.95** each	$_____
☐	*UNIVERSAL WISDOM* (Hardback) at **$49.95** each	$_____
☐	*BUSINESS OWNERS' WISDOM* (Hardback) at **$49.95** each	$_____
☐	*BUSINESS OWNERS' WISDOM* (Soft Cover) at **$39.95** each*	$_____
☐	*ORDERS OF 10 OR MORE SOFT COVERS at $**19.95** each	$_____
	*ORDERS OF 100 OR MORE SOFT COVERS at $**10.00** each	$_____
	Postage and handling at **$8.00** per book (Allow 21 days delivery)	$_____
	TOTAL PAYMENT	$_____

POST TO:

Clown Publishing, PO Box 1764, North Sydney NSW 2059, Australia
T 02 9923 0800 F 02 9923 0888 E brett@kellypartners.com.au
www.brettkelly.com.au